The Heart's Ledger

Reconciling Emotional Debts and Investing in Relationships

By

OLUSIJI ADENIYI

ParadigmShift Publishing LLC
Colorado Springs, Colorado USA

The Heart's Ledger:
Reconciling Emotional Debts and Investing in Relationships

Copyright © 2025 by Olusiji Adeniyi.

All rights reserved. No part of this book may be reproduced, stored in a retrieval system, or transmitted in any form or by any means—electronic, mechanical, photocopying, recording, or otherwise—without the prior written permission of the publisher, except for brief quotations in critical reviews and articles.

Printed in the United States of America.

Published by

ParadigmShift Publishing LLC
Colorado Springs, Colorado USA.

https://www.paradigmShiftPublishingllc.com

Book Design & Cover Design by Paradigm Patterns

ISBN - Paperback: 979-8-9922974-5-4

ISBN - Hardcover: 979-8-9922974-4-7

First Edition: 1st March 2025

Library of Congress Control Number: 2025933775

Rights and Permissions Notice

For permissions, inquiries, or bulk purchases, contact:
insights@paradigmshiftpublishingllc.com

If you believe this book has been reproduced or distributed without permission, please report violations to the publisher at insights@paradigmshiftpublishingllc.com

Legal Disclaimer

This is a non-fiction work. Every effort has been made to ensure the accuracy of the information provided. However, the author and publisher assume no responsibility for errors or omissions. The opinions expressed are those of the author and do not necessarily reflect those of the publisher. This book is not intended as a substitute for professional advice. Readers should consult appropriate professionals before making any decisions based on the contents of this book.

Publisher's Note

The content of The Heart's Ledger: Reconciling Emotional Debts and Investing in Relationships, is based on extensive research, professional experience, and personal insight. While the author has made every effort to provide accurate and up-to-date information, knowledge evolves, and interpretations may vary. Readers are encouraged to approach the material critically and apply discernment in its use.

This book is meant to inspire, educate, and provoke thought. The ideas presented should be explored in context, and readers should seek additional perspectives when necessary.

Dedication

To my beloved wife Modupe,
Radiant jewel of my heart
Your love illuminates my world.

With eternal gratitude and devotion,
Olusiji

About the Author

Olusiji Adeniyi is an accomplished human resources specialist and an authority on optimizing human potential. With decades of expertise, he seamlessly integrates personal transformation, financial independence, and relational accountability. In his role as a military instructor focused on logistics, Olusiji embodies strategy, discipline, and leadership—principles that profoundly influence his written work.

Rooted in rich Yoruba intellectual traditions and raised by British-educated parents, Olusiji fuses African wisdom, Western pragmatism, and a profound grasp of human nature. His mission is to illuminate the unseen emotional, financial, and metaphysical forces that shape our lives, challenge limiting narratives and empower individuals to reclaim authorship over their destinies.

In *The Heart's Ledger: Reconciling Emotional Debts and Investing in Relationships*, Olusiji distills decades of research, observation, and lived experiences to reveal how unresolved trauma, inherited beliefs, and unconscious patterns dictate relationships and life choices. His work guides readers toward conscious reconciliation, enabling them to embrace love, purpose, and prosperity with clarity and intention.

Beyond writing, Olusiji enjoys music, chess, intellectual discourse, and family life. His work in financial education and wealth-building continues to empower and uplift his readers towards transforming emotional and financial debts into lasting legacies of abundance.

Acknowledgments

To God Almighty—the inexhaustible source of all that was, all that is, and all that will ever be—I owe everything.

The Architect of existence, the Keeper of time, the Author of wisdom—You have been my compass, my anchor, my wellspring of grace. Without You, there is no voice, no vision, no story to tell.

To my parents, whose lives were my first lessons in steadfast, unconditional love, I am forever grateful.

Your unwavering belief in me has been the quiet force behind every step I take.

To my family, friends, and loved ones, thank you for your relentless generosity of spirit. In moments of joy, in seasons of challenge, your tireless love has been my most valuable possession.

This book is but a reflection of what you have all poured into me. I am grateful in ways words can never fully express.

Contents

Dedication 4

About the Author 5

Acknowledgments 6

Foreword 13

Introduction: The Emotional Economy 14

1. Roots of Emotional Debt 20
2. Adolescent Accounts—The Formative Years 25
3. Early Adulthood—The First Major Audits 30
4. Midlife Reckonings—Balancing the Books 35
5. The Golden Years & Legacy: Emotional Estate Planning 41
6. Identifying Emotional Creditors & Debtors 47
7. Strategies for Emotional Debt Repayment 54
8. Healing Emotional Bankruptcy 60
9. Building Emotional Wealth —Investing in Emotional Capital 67
10. Navigating Emotional Mergers & Acquisitions 73
11. The Art of Emotional Budgeting 79
12. Diversifying Your Emotional Portfolio 86
13. Emotional Entrepreneurship 93
14. Emotional Sustainability 100
15. Emotional Wealth Ahead —The Future of Emotional Wealth 106

16. Conclusion: Balancing the Ledger, Enriching Life 112

Glossary 121

References 127

Index...129

Introduction: The Emotional Economy

This section introduces the "hidden ledger of the heart," revealing how emotional transactions shape relationships. It explores unresolved issues from the past and their influence on present connections. By understanding emotional debts, credits, and their impact, readers gain tools for fostering trust, healing wounds, and achieving emotional prosperity.

Chapter 1: Roots of Emotional Debt

Childhood experiences lay the groundwork for our emotional patterns. Parental influences, sibling bonds, and early friendships create the first entries in our emotional ledger. This chapter encourages readers to examine these formative imprints, uncover their effects, and address the emotional debts that shape adult connections.

Chapter 2: Adolescent Accounts

Adolescence introduces turbulent emotional trades, from peer pressure to first love. Identity formation and social challenges leave lasting marks on emotional behavior. This chapter examines how teenage experiences shape self-worth, relational habits, and coping mechanisms, offering readers insight into these critical years.

Chapter 3: Early Adulthood Audits

Early adulthood is a time of emotional reckoning, balancing career ambitions, romantic risks, and evolving friendships. This chapter explores the impact of pivotal decisions and inherited family patterns. Readers are guided to reassess emotional investments and establish healthy practices for trust and connection.

Chapter 4: Midlife Adjustments

Midlife calls for a reassessment of priorities. Career crossroads, parenting challenges, and personal crises prompt reflection on emotional portfolios. This chapter emphasizes reshaping relationships, fostering resilience, and reimagining goals during this transformative stage of life.

Chapter 5: Golden Years and Legacies

Later life invites renewal and reflection. Retirement offers space for self-discovery, grandparenting provides generational giving, and loss demands emotional resilience. This chapter highlights building meaningful connections, embracing closure, and leaving a legacy of emotional prosperity.

Chapter 6: Mapping Emotional Debts

Identifying emotional creditors and debtors begins with mapping emotional networks. This chapter examines patterns of giving and taking, highlighting the unseen costs of emotional deficits. By accurately valuing emotional assets, readers learn to reconcile relationships and restore balance.

Chapter 7: Repaying Emotional Debts

True healing involves addressing emotional debts through apologies, forgiveness, and restorative actions. This chapter offers strategies to mend broken bonds, foster self-forgiveness, and create space for renewed trust. Readers are encouraged to rebuild relationships with intentional care.

Chapter 8: Recovering from Depletion

Emotional bankruptcy, marked by depleted reserves, requires structured recovery. This chapter outlines steps to recognize exhaustion, rebuild self-worth, and seek professional guidance. Readers are encouraged to prioritize self-care and resilience to restore emotional stability.

Chapter 9: Investing in Emotional Wealth

This chapter explores empathy, vulnerability, trust, and gratitude as key emotional assets. By making intentional investments in these traits, readers can strengthen relationships, foster resilience, and build a foundation of lasting emotional prosperity.

Chapter 10: Navigating Emotional Integration

Modern relationships often involve blending families, navigating cultural divides, and managing digital bonds. This chapter provides strategies for integrating emotional worlds with balance and empathy, fostering harmony across diverse connections.

Chapter 11: Mastering Emotional Budgets

Emotional budgeting involves allocating energy wisely by setting boundaries and fostering equity. This chapter highlights intentional spending of emotional resources to maintain balance and ensure relationships and self-care are mutually enriching.

Chapter 12: Diversifying Emotional Investments

Diversifying emotional portfolios ensures resilience and adaptability. This chapter emphasizes broadening relationships, balancing risks with stability, and preparing for crises to strengthen emotional security and growth over time.

Chapter 13: Emotional Innovation

This chapter examines opportunities for emotional growth through innovation and creativity in relationships. By balancing risk and reward in deep connections, readers learn to expand emotional networks with purpose and foster meaningful bonds.

Chapter 14: Sustaining Emotional Growth

Sustaining emotional wealth requires cultivating joy as a renewable resource, practicing ethical giving, and fostering ripple effects of growth. This chapter provides a long-term blueprint for maintaining balance, harmony, and emotional prosperity.

Chapter 15: The Future of Emotional Wealth

The final chapter explores emerging trends in human connection, from digital tools to global cultural unity. It emphasizes lifelong growth, adaptability, and creating a legacy of meaningful relationships that enrich both personal and collective well-being.

Conclusion: Finalizing the Emotional Ledger

The conclusion reflects on the ongoing journey of reconciling emotional debts and fostering growth. Readers are encouraged to leave a legacy of meaningful connections while embracing self-awareness and emotional prosperity as lifelong pursuits.

Foreword

I've had the privilege of knowing Olusiji for most of my life. As family and a lifelong friend, I've admired his dedication to understanding human connections.

Through shared conversations, joys, and challenges, Olusiji's gift for transforming life's complexities into lessons of compassion, resilience, and growth stands out.

His book, *The Heart's Ledger: Reconciling Emotional Debts and Investing in Relationships*, reflects his belief in the transformative power of relationships and emotional integrity. Combining personal insights and research, it offers wisdom for healing wounds, strengthening bonds, and navigating emotions.

What makes this book special is its balance of wisdom and practicality. Olusiji lives these principles daily, rooted in empathy and authenticity, believing emotional prosperity is attainable for all.

This isn't just a book, it's an invitation to reflect, grow, and build a meaningful, connected life. It's a testament to Olusiji's mission to illuminate the intricacies of our shared humanity. I'm honored to introduce this labor of love and its transformative journey.

With warmth and appreciation,

Ope Adeleke
(Acclaimed Author of *The Book on Self-Discovery*).
Ontario, Canada.

INTRODUCTION

The Emotional Economy

Every relationship operates within an unspoken system of emotional exchanges. These transactions, much like a financial ledger, form the foundation of how we connect, build trust, and navigate conflicts. Yet, unlike monetary dealings, emotional exchanges often go unnoticed. They accumulate silently, shaping the patterns of our relationships and, ultimately, our lives.

This book begins with a transformative truth: our emotional issues predate our existing relationships. The unresolved imbalances from our past influence how we engage with others today, often without our awareness. By exploring these dynamics, we uncover the hidden ledger of the heart, a framework that helps us reconcile past emotional debts and foster prosperity in our present and future connections.

Unveiling the Hidden Ledger

Imagine your emotional life as a ledger, meticulously recording every significant interaction. Each moment of kindness, support, or betrayal leaves an entry. Some interactions act as deposits—enriching your emotional reserves. Others, like betrayals or neglect, create debts that linger, unacknowledged yet profoundly impactful.

These entries form the emotional blueprint of our lives, beginning in childhood. A parent's affection might instill confidence, while their absence could leave a deficit of self-worth. Early friendships, sibling dynamics, and formative experiences write the first chapters of this ledger. However, these entries are not just historical, they actively shape how we interpret and respond to new relationships.

For example, a person who experienced conditional love as a child may struggle to accept unconditional support as an adult. Their ledger, influenced by past experiences, colors their perception of current interactions. The unresolved "debt" of unmet needs from childhood often manifests as insecurity, distrust, or self-sabotage in relationships.

Understanding the hidden ledger of the heart allows us to take the first step toward healing. By acknowledging these imbalances, we gain clarity on how past entries shape current behaviors. The ledger may not lie, but it can be reconciled.

The Currency of Feelings

At the core of the heart's ledger lies the currency of emotions. Trust, empathy, love, and patience enrich relationships, while resentment, neglect, and betrayal deplete them. Unlike financial transactions, emotional exchanges are complex and influenced by history and perception.

Consider how a simple compliment might feel like a small deposit to someone with a secure sense of self. To another person, starved of validation, that same compliment might feel like a profound act of generosity. Similarly, a thoughtless remark from a loved one might barely register for some but cut deeply for those carrying unresolved pain from past relationships.

These exchanges form the fabric of our emotional economy, yet they are often invisible. We may not realize how unresolved grief from a childhood loss affects our ability to trust or how years of unspoken resentment toward a parent shape our responses to others.

This lack of awareness can lead to irrational decisions— pushing away those who offer genuine care or clinging to relationships that deplete our reserves.

The goal of this book is to illuminate these invisible balances. By understanding how emotional transactions operate, we can begin to recognize the patterns in our relationships and address the imbalances that hold us back.

Emotional Transactions: Recognizing Their Worth

Every emotional act holds intrinsic value. A kind gesture deposits goodwill, while neglect withdraws trust. Yet, without conscious acknowledgment of these transactions, relationships risk imbalance and misunderstanding.

Imagine a partnership where one person consistently gives more—offering support, love, and effort—while the other remains distant or indifferent. The giver might feel drained, perceiving the imbalance as neglect. The receiver, unaware of this dynamic, might view the relationship as stable. These unspoken tallies create tension, often surfacing as resentment or conflict.

Recognizing the worth of emotional transactions begins with naming them. Acknowledging the significance of apologies, acts of patience, or moments of vulnerability creates accountability. This practice not only fosters healthier interpersonal exchanges but also strengthens the relationship we have with ourselves. Self-compassion replenishes emotional reserves, while self-criticism erodes them. By treating ourselves with care, we enhance our capacity to engage in balanced, fulfilling relationships.

Balancing Emotional Books

Why does balancing our emotional books matter? Because unresolved debts do not disappear—they accumulate. Like interest on an unpaid loan, emotional imbalances compound over time, influencing our behaviors and perceptions in ways we may not fully understand.

Consider someone who never resolved feelings of abandonment. They might approach relationships with defensiveness, preemptively distancing themselves to avoid the pain of being left again. Similarly, a person who internalized criticism as a child might develop perfectionistic tendencies, constantly seeking validation to counteract feelings of inadequacy.

Balancing emotional books begins with awareness—acknowledging the debts we carry and tracing their origins. This requires honest reflection, free of judgment or shame. From there, it involves deliberate action: making amends where possible, forgiving past mistakes, and setting boundaries to protect our emotional reserves.

However, emotional reconciliation is not solely about addressing the past—it is also about investing in the future. Just as financial stability involves saving and investing, emotional prosperity requires cultivating habits and relationships that yield long-term fulfillment. This includes developing empathy, practicing gratitude, and embracing vulnerability.

Emotional Accounting and Relationship Health

Emotional accounting, the practice of tracking and balancing emotional exchanges—is essential for healthy relationships. It is not about keeping score but about fostering mutual respect and understanding.

In friendships or partnerships, unspoken grievances often lead to erosion of trust. For instance, one friend may feel undervalued if their efforts are consistently overlooked, while the other, unaware of this perception, remains oblivious. Over time, this imbalance fosters resentment, eventually straining the relationship.

By practicing emotional accounting, we bring clarity to these dynamics. This involves reflecting on critical questions: Are we giving more than we receive? Are we neglecting to acknowledge others' contributions? Are old wounds shaping how we perceive current interactions? These insights allow us to address imbalances before they escalate.

Moreover, emotional accounting illuminates inherited patterns. Many of us unconsciously replicate the dynamics we observed in childhood—whether through self-criticism that echoes a parent's voice or through attachment styles shaped by early experiences. By auditing these patterns, we gain the tools to break cycles that no longer serve us.

Toward Emotional Prosperity

The heart's ledger is not just a record of the past—it is a map for the future. By reconciling old debts and fostering intentional emotional investments, we create space for growth, fulfillment, and connection.

This book offers a roadmap for navigating this journey. The first section, *Auditing the Past*, explores how childhood, adolescence, and early adulthood shape emotional patterns. By understanding these origins, readers can begin to identify the imbalances influencing their relationships.

The second section, *Reconciliation and Healing*, provides practical strategies for addressing unresolved issues. Through forgiveness, restorative actions, and self-compassion, readers learn how to mend fractures in their emotional ledger and rebuild trust in themselves and others.

The final section, *Building Emotional Prosperity*, shifts focus to growth and sustainability. Readers discover how to invest in meaningful relationships, balance emotional resources, and cultivate habits that foster long-term fulfillment.

A New Lens on Relationships

The Heart's Ledger invites readers to view their relationships through a transformative lens. By understanding the emotional economy, we can rewrite the narratives that limit us and step into connections with clarity, compassion, and intention.

Our issues may predate our existing relationships, but they do not have to define them. Each reconciled debt, each intentional investment, moves us closer to a legacy of emotional prosperity— one that enriches not just our own lives but also the lives of those we touch.

As you begin this journey, think of yourself as the book-keeper of your emotional wealth. Take stock of your past entries, reconcile imbalances, and invest in a future rich in connection and meaning. Let this book be your guide as you embark on the path toward healing, growth, and lasting emotional prosperity.

CHAPTER 1

Roots of Emotional Debt

Childhood is where our emotional lives begin. It is in these formative years that the seeds of our emotional identity are planted. Parents, siblings, and peers shape the foundation of our inner world, leaving imprints that echo throughout adulthood. These early experiences teach us how to interpret love, trust, and belonging, and they leave an indelible mark on the ledger of our hearts.

This chapter explores the roles of caregivers, family dynamics, and friendships in crafting our earliest emotional blueprints. By unearthing the foundations of our emotional debt, we begin to understand how unresolved patterns affect our adult relationships.

Emotional Roots: Early Life Imprints

From the moment we enter the world, our experiences shape how we connect. An infant does not understand language but learns quickly from interactions. A soothing touch fosters security, neglect fosters fear. These early moments create a framework for how we relate to others.

Imagine a child who cries and is comforted. That child internalizes a sense of safety and trust. Contrast this with a child whose cries go unanswered, who learns that vulnerability is dangerous, and needs may not be met. These lessons don't disappear, they form the subconscious scripts we follow in relationships.

Psychologists refer to these patterns as attachment styles: secure, anxious, avoidant, or disorganized. Each style originates from how caregivers responded to our emotional needs. A secure attachment fosters confidence in relationships, while avoidant or anxious patterns can lead to challenges in trust or intimacy. These early imprints shape how we navigate connections long after childhood ends.

The Ledger of Parental Influence

Parents are our first emotional creditors. Their love, attention, and guidance are the first deposits into our emotional accounts. However, even the most loving parents can unintentionally leave emotional debts.

For example, a parent who struggles to express affection may leave a child feeling unseen, even if love is present.

Conversely, a parent who overcompensates may unintentionally foster dependence, making it difficult for the child to develop autonomy. These experiences influence how we view ourselves and approach relationships later in life.

To reconcile this part of the emotional ledger, it is essential to approach it with compassion. Parents are shaped by their own histories, often passing down unresolved patterns. Recognizing these influences allows us to break cycles without assigning blame. By understanding how our caregivers shaped us, we can begin to rewrite inherited narratives and foster healthier relationships.

Parental Roles in Emotional Growth

Parents teach us how to navigate emotions, often without realizing it. Their actions, whether nurturing or dismissive— become the models we carry into adulthood. A parent who validates emotions teaches resilience, while one who avoids conflict might instill a fear of confrontation.

Consider the impact of a parent's response to a tantrum. A calm, patient approach teaches that emotions are manageable and not shameful. On the other hand, dismissiveness might teach that feelings are unwelcome or burdensome. These lessons become the foundation of our inner emotional dialogue.

Beyond direct interactions, parents set examples for love and partnership. A child who witnesses respect and communication in a marriage absorbs those behaviors. Conversely, a child who sees conflict or neglect may normalize dysfunction. These templates influence the expectations we bring to our own relationships.

Sibling Bonds: Support or Strain

Siblings often serve as our first peers, teaching us about competition, collaboration, and boundaries. These relationships can be a source of support or a source of tension, leaving deep marks on our emotional development.

In harmonious sibling dynamics, children learn loyalty and teamwork. A protective older sibling might foster feelings of safety, while shared experiences create bonds of trust. However, rivalry or favoritism can introduce insecurity. A child who feels overshadowed by a sibling might carry feelings of inadequacy into adulthood.

Even the absence of siblings shapes emotional growth.

Only children, for instance, often develop deep independence but may struggle with collaboration. Understanding the dynamics of sibling relationships helps us recognize patterns that affect how we connect with others in adulthood.

Youthful Friendships: First Emotional Trades

Beyond family, friendships introduce children to the broader emotional economy. These early relationships are where children learn trust, reciprocity, and loyalty. Positive friendships teach collaboration and empathy, while negative experiences can instill caution or distrust.

Consider the child who is excluded from a group. That experience might lead to a lifelong fear of rejection. Conversely, a friend who offers kindness during a tough time creates a sense of security that can resonate for years. These early trades—both deposits and withdrawals—shape how we approach adult relationships.

Reflecting on youthful friendships helps us identify patterns we may unconsciously repeat. Were our early relationships based on mutual respect, or were they imbalanced? By examining these dynamics, we can better understand the emotional templates we bring to adult friendships.

Tracing the Ripples

The imprints of childhood—whether from parents, siblings, or friends—do not stay confined to the past. They ripple forward, influencing our approach to love, trust, and even conflict resolution. Understanding these patterns gives us the power to rewrite them.

For instance, someone who grew up feeling unworthy might seek constant validation in relationships. Recognizing this as a response to childhood neglect allows them to address the root cause. Similarly, a person who fears intimacy due to early betrayals can begin to take small steps toward trust.

Auditing these early experiences is not about blaming the past but about understanding it. This awareness empowers us to make intentional choices, breaking free from cycles that no longer serve us.

Rewriting the Emotional Ledger

Excavating childhood imprints is a courageous act. It requires confronting painful truths but offers the promise of liberation. By identifying the entries in our emotional ledger, we gain the clarity needed to move forward with intention.

Rewriting these entries does not mean erasing them.

Instead, it involves reframing them with compassion— understanding that the wounds we carry often reflect the limitations of those who shaped us. This process allows us to challenge harmful narratives and replace them with healthier patterns.

For example, someone who internalized a message of unworthiness might seek out affirming relationships that challenge that belief. By consciously choosing experiences that deposit emotional wealth, we create a new balance in our ledger—one built on trust, reciprocity, and mutual respect.

Moving Forward

Childhood imprints are profound but not permanent. By examining the foundations of our emotional debt, we reclaim the power to shape our future. This chapter lays the groundwork for deeper exploration, offering insight into how our early experiences intertwine with later stages of life.

As we move forward in this book, we will build on this understanding, exploring how adolescence, adulthood, and beyond offer opportunities to reconcile old debts and cultivate emotional wealth. Our past shapes us, but it does not define us. By auditing the roots of our emotional ledger, we take the first step toward lasting growth and connection.

CHAPTER 2

Adolescent Accounts—The Formative Years

Adolescence is a period of profound transformation, where identities are created, emotional patterns take shape, and the heart's ledger grows exponentially. During these formative years, the influence of peers, the exhilaration of first loves, academic pressures, and the search for identity converge to create a potent emotional mix. These experiences, though transient, leave lasting imprints, shaping how we approach relationships and challenges in adulthood.

This chapter explores the emotional dynamics of adolescence, examining how unresolved debts from this stage continue to influence our relationships, decisions, and sense of self.

Peer Pressure and Emotional Balance

During adolescence, peer groups often replace family as the central source of validation and belonging. Acceptance becomes the currency of emotional transactions, while rejection exacts a steep toll. Teens are especially vulnerable to peer pressure, as the need to fit in frequently outweighs the desire to remain authentic.

For some, peer groups provide a haven, fostering connection and confidence. But for others, the pressure to conform to group norms can lead to internal conflict. A teen might suppress their interests or beliefs to gain acceptance, leaving behind a residue of self-betrayal. Conversely, those excluded or bullied may develop feelings of shame, alienation, or worthlessness that persist long into adulthood.

These early social dynamics establish patterns of emotional exchange. Moments of inclusion deposit confidence and self-worth, while rejection or humiliation depletes emotional reserves. Adolescents who develop resilience—balancing the need for belonging with self-assurance—carry this strength into adulthood. In contrast, those who struggle to navigate peer pressure may find themselves prioritizing external approval over personal values, a pattern that often repeats in adult relationships.

Young Love: Borrowing Emotional Wealth

Few experiences are as intense or impactful as first love. For many, adolescence is the first time they open their hearts fully to another person, experiencing vulnerability and intimacy in new and profound ways. These early romances can feel like emotional windfalls, offering euphoria and affirmation. However, they also carry significant risks, often leaving lingering debts.

In young love, teens often "borrow" emotional wealth from their partners. They derive a sense of identity, validation, and worth through the relationship. For instance, a kind word from a significant other might feel like a deposit of self-worth, while criticism or indifference can create deep wounds. These transactions, however unbalanced, lay the foundation for how we perceive and navigate romantic relationships.

When young love ends, as it often does, heartbreak can feel catastrophic. For some, the pain of loss becomes a lesson in resilience, fostering independence and emotional maturity. For others, it reinforces fears of vulnerability, leading to guardedness in future relationships. Revisiting these early romances allows us to identify the patterns and beliefs they instilled, helping us to rewrite narratives that no longer serve us.

Academic Demands: Emotional Stress Loads

Adolescence is not only a time of social and romantic exploration but also one of significant academic pressure. For many, school becomes a proving ground where self-worth is tied to grades, achievements, and accolades. Success feels like a deposit in the emotional ledger, while failure withdraws from it.

High-achieving students may internalize the belief that their value lies in performance, fostering perfectionism and anxiety. Conversely, those who struggle academically often carry feelings of inadequacy or shame, equating academic setbacks with personal failure. These patterns, once established, frequently persist into adulthood, influencing how individuals approach challenges and setbacks in other areas of life.

Supportive figures—whether parents, teachers, or mentors—play a crucial role during this stage. Encouragement and understanding can help mitigate the emotional toll of academic pressures, fostering resilience and self-confidence. Conversely, criticism or unrealistic expectations can exacerbate feelings of inadequacy, leaving lasting imprints on the emotional ledger.

Identity Formation: A Personal Audit

Perhaps the most defining task of adolescence is identity formation. This stage is marked by questions of self-discovery: Who am I? What do I value? Where do I belong? These questions are not just intellectual; they are deeply emotional, tied to one's sense of worth and belonging.

For many teens, identity exploration involves trying on different roles and personas. They experiment with interests, peer groups, and personal styles, searching for authenticity. However, external pressures—whether societal, familial, or cultural—can complicate this process. Teens from marginalized communities, for instance, often face the added burden of navigating societal biases while forming their sense of self.

The struggle to balance personal and social identities often leaves unresolved conflicts. A teen who suppresses their individuality to please others may carry feelings of inauthenticity into adulthood. Similarly, someone who faced criticism for their choices might internalize self-doubt, making it difficult to assert themselves later in life.

Revisiting this phase of life with curiosity and compassion allows us to audit the beliefs and patterns formed during this time. By examining which aspects of our identity feel authentic and which were shaped by external pressures, we can begin to align more closely with our true selves.

Tracing the Adolescent Imprint

The emotional experiences of adolescence leave a lasting imprint on the heart's ledger. Rejection, betrayal, success, and connection from this period ripple forward, influencing how we approach relationships and challenges in adulthood. These patterns, while deeply ingrained, are not immutable.

For example, a person who felt ostracized in their teens might struggle with imposter syndrome in the workplace, constantly doubting their worth. Someone who faced betrayal in young love may approach future relationships with suspicion, making it difficult to build trust. By identifying the origins of these patterns, we can begin to address them and move forward with greater clarity and intention.

Breaking free from these cycles requires honest reflection. Revisiting adolescent experiences is not about assigning blame but about understanding their impact. Awareness allows us to rewrite these narratives, transforming old wounds into opportunities for growth.

Revisiting Adolescent Accounts

Adolescence is often romanticized as a time of freedom and possibility, but for many, it is also a period marked by insecurity and upheaval. Revisiting this chapter of life can be uncomfortable, requiring us to confront painful memories and acknowledge their ongoing influence. Yet this process is essential for healing and growth.

By examining the entries in our adolescent ledger—both positive and negative—we gain insight into the patterns that shape our current relationships. We can identify opportunities for reconciliation, whether by forgiving ourselves for past mistakes or mending fractured connections from our youth.

Ultimately, adolescence is not just a chapter in our life story; it is a foundation for everything that comes after. By auditing this part of our ledger with honesty and compassion, we can build a future rooted in clarity, intention, and emotional balance.

Moving Forward

The adolescent years are a crucible of emotional growth.

The lessons learned during this time—whether through peer interactions, first loves, academic challenges, or identity exploration—shape the patterns and beliefs that guide us into adulthood. These experiences, while formative, are not definitive.

Auditing the adolescent accounts in our emotional ledger offers a chance to reconcile unresolved debts and rewrite narratives that no longer serve us. By doing so, we create a foundation for healthier relationships, greater self-awareness, and a richer emotional life.

As we move forward, the lessons of adolescence become tools for growth, helping us navigate the complexities of adult relationships with clarity and confidence. Our past may shape us, but it does not have to define us.

CHAPTER 3

Early Adulthood—The First Major Audits

Early adulthood is a pivotal stage in emotional development, where the choices we make in careers, relationships, and personal growth intersect with the unresolved patterns of childhood and adolescence. This period often serves as the first major "audit" of our emotional ledger, requiring us to assess how past imprints shape our present decisions. The experiences of early adulthood set the foundation for future growth, introducing both challenges and opportunities for reconciliation and enrichment.

This chapter delves into the transitions of early adulthood, exploring the dynamics of career choices, romantic relationships, evolving friendships, and family patterns. It examines how these new "accounts" interact with existing debts and credits, offering insights into how individuals can navigate this transformative period with clarity and intention.

College and Career: New Accounts Opened

The transition into adulthood is marked by independence and exploration. Whether through higher education, starting a career, or pursuing other paths, early adulthood presents opportunities to redefine ourselves. However, these new beginnings are often shadowed by the unresolved patterns of our past.

Career: The Test of Self-Worth

For many, a career becomes an external measure of value.

Promotions, achievements, and financial success are seen as deposits into the emotional ledger, while setbacks and failures are perceived as withdrawals. These experiences often mirror unresolved dynamics from childhood.

For example, someone who grew up equating love with achievement may feel driven to overperform, seeking validation through professional success. Conversely, those who internalized self-doubt as children may struggle with imposter syndrome, doubting their competence despite evidence to the contrary.

Thriving in this domain requires decoupling self-worth from external outcomes. Reframing setbacks as opportunities for growth, rather than reflections of personal failure, allows for a more balanced and resilient approach to career challenges.

Education: A Stage for Reinvention

For those entering college, this phase often represents a chance to reinvent oneself. Free from the constraints of childhood roles and expectations, young adults can explore new identities and passions. However, the freedom to make choices also brings risks, as unresolved insecurities from adolescence may resurface.

A student may struggle with the pressure to meet high expectations, feeling the weight of past patterns. Recognizing these influences and addressing them with self-awareness can help individuals navigate this transformative period with greater confidence.

Romantic Entanglements: Merging Emotional Assets

In early adulthood, romantic relationships take on a new depth, often serving as a mirror to past experiences. These relationships are not just about love—they are about merging emotional assets such as trust, vulnerability, and commitment.

The Allure of Intimacy

Early romantic bonds often feel like uncharted territory, offering the possibility of deep connection. However, they also expose vulnerabilities shaped by unresolved debts from childhood and adolescence. For example, a person who experienced conditional love as a child might seek reassurance in relationships, while someone who learned to suppress emotions may struggle to open up.

Patterns from the Past

The dynamics of early romantic relationships often reflect earlier experiences. A partner's criticism might echo a parent's disapproval, or a fear of abandonment may resurface during conflicts. These patterns, if left unexamined, can lead to cycles of misunderstanding and pain.

Rewriting the Script

Recognizing these patterns is the first step toward healing.

Early adult relationships offer opportunities to challenge past narratives and build healthier connections. By embracing vulnerability and addressing fears, individuals can transform these partnerships into sources of growth rather than conflict.

Evolving Friendships: Reassessing Long-Term Investments

Friendships undergo significant shifts in early adulthood.

The bonds formed during adolescence are tested by changing priorities, new environments, and personal growth.

The Value of Lifelong Bonds

Some friendships deepen during this stage, offering stability and support amid life's changes. These connections are emotional assets, enriching the ledger with trust, encouragement, and shared experiences. However, maintaining these bonds requires intentional effort, as busy schedules and competing demands can strain even the strongest relationships.

Letting Go of Emotional Liabilities

Not all friendships endure. Some, while meaningful in their time, may become draining or unbalanced as life evolves. A friend who once provided support may grow distant, critical, or unsupportive. Letting go of these connections is often necessary for emotional well-being, freeing energy for relationships that align with one's values and aspirations.

By assessing friendships honestly, individuals can focus on nurturing meaningful connections while releasing those that no longer serve their emotional growth.

Family Patterns: Debt Reconciliation

As young adults gain independence, their relationships with family members often come under scrutiny. This stage offers an opportunity to renegotiate inherited emotional debts and establish healthier dynamics.

Recognizing Emotional Inheritance

Many of the emotional patterns carried into adulthood originate within the family. Parental criticism, sibling rivalry, or unspoken expectations shape our earliest perceptions of love, trust, and belonging. These imprints often resurface in new forms during early adulthood, influencing how we approach relationships and challenges.

Setting Boundaries

Independence allows individuals to establish boundaries with family members, particularly in cases of toxic or enmeshed dynamics. Boundaries are not acts of rejection—they are affirmations of one's needs and values.

For example, limiting contact with a controlling parent can preserve autonomy and emotional health, even if it provokes conflict initially.

Reconciliation and Healing

For some, early adulthood is also a time to seek closure and reconciliation. Addressing unresolved conflicts or acknowledging past wounds can foster healing, both for the individual and their family members. Approaching these conversations with empathy and intention creates space for understanding and growth.

Revisiting Early Adulthood Accounts

Early adulthood is a time of significant change and growth.

It is a period where individuals begin taking ownership of their emotional ledger, assessing which patterns to keep and which to release.

This stage offers an opportunity to reflect on new experiences, recognize the influence of past imprints, and make intentional choices. By revisiting early adulthood accounts with honesty and compassion, individuals can identify areas for growth and create a foundation for lasting emotional prosperity.

Moving Forward

The experiences of early adulthood—new careers, romantic relationships, evolving friendships, and shifting family dynamics—serve as a crucible for emotional growth. They challenge us to confront unresolved debts, embrace vulnerability, and invest in connections that enrich our lives.

By auditing the emotional ledger during this stage, we gain clarity and agency, allowing us to build a future defined by resilience, connection, and fulfillment. As we move into the next chapter, we will explore how these lessons evolve in midlife, offering new opportunities for reconciliation and growth.

CHAPTER 4

Midlife Reckonings—Balancing the Books

Midlife is a period of reflection and recalibration. The decisions and patterns established in earlier years come under scrutiny as individuals assess their accomplishments, relationships, and aspirations. Often described as a crossroads, this stage brings opportunities to reassess priorities, confront unresolved emotional debts, and lay the groundwork for the next phase of life.

This chapter explores four critical dimensions of midlife reckoning: career choices, the emotional toll of divorce, parenting as a platform for teaching emotional values, and the midlife crisis as a catalyst for redefining emotional priorities. Each section examines how these experiences reshape the heart's ledger, offering paths for growth and fulfillment.

Career Choices: Loss or Gain

For many, careers define not only professional success but also identity and self-worth. By midlife, however, the toll of relentless ambition or unfulfilled aspirations becomes clearer. The ledger of professional life reflects both rewards and sacrifices, prompting a reevaluation of emotional investments.

The Illusion of Success

In youth, success is often measured by external achievements—promotions, income, and accolades. By midlife, these accomplishments may feel hollow if they have come at the expense of personal well-being or meaningful relationships.

Consider the professional who prioritized work over family, only to find themselves isolated despite their achievements. The emotional ledger reveals entries not just of success but also of missed opportunities for connection and fulfillment.

Reclaiming Purpose

Midlife offers a chance to redefine what success means. For some, this involves pivoting to roles that align with personal values, such as pursuing creative passions or engaging in community work. For others, it means reevaluating work-life balance, setting boundaries, or finding purpose in their current role.

This reassessment transforms the career ledger into a tool for intentional growth, where losses become lessons and gains provide the confidence to embrace new directions.

Marriage and Divorce: Splitting Emotional Assets

Long-term relationships, including marriages, undergo significant scrutiny in midlife. The cumulative emotional exchanges within these partnerships often come to the forefront, forcing individuals to confront imbalances, unmet needs, or unspoken grievances.

The Weight of Emotional Assets

Marriage is one of life's most significant mergers of emotional resources. Over time, the balance of trust, affection, and support can shift. Some couples navigate these changes together, while others find themselves drifting apart.

In many cases, unresolved issues from earlier years resurface with greater intensity. The shared ledger of the relationship may reveal entries of resentment, neglect, or unaddressed conflict, creating a reckoning point for both partners.

Divorce: Emotional Debts and Renewal

For some, divorce becomes the only viable resolution to an unbalanced partnership. While painful, it offers an opportunity to untangle emotional assets and reassess individual needs. The process of separating shared dreams and trust can feel like emotional bankruptcy, but it also provides space for healing and growth.

Rebuilding after divorce involves confronting personal patterns and taking responsibility for one's contributions to the relationship's dynamics. By addressing these issues with honesty and compassion, individuals can approach future relationships with greater clarity and intention.

Parenthood: Teaching Emotional Values

Midlife often coincides with children transitioning into adolescence or adulthood. Parenting during this stage brings its own challenges and rewards, as parents navigate shifting dynamics and impart values that shape the next generation's emotional wealth.

The Mirror of Parenthood

Children reflect their parents' strengths and weaknesses, offering a unique lens through which to examine emotional patterns. For example, a parent's impatience might manifest in a child's behavior, while their resilience inspires similar traits.

Parenting forces individuals to confront their own emotional legacies. A parent who experienced criticism in childhood may inadvertently replicate that dynamic or, conversely, overcompensate by avoiding conflict. Recognizing these patterns creates an opportunity to break cycles and model healthier behaviors.

Balancing Sacrifice and Self-Care

Parenting demands immense emotional investment, often requiring parents to juggle competing priorities, such as careers and aging parents. Striking a balance between caregiving and self-care is essential for maintaining emotional health.

By modeling empathy, communication, and self-compassion, parents teach their children essential emotional skills. These lessons form the foundation of emotional resilience, creating a ripple effect that extends beyond the immediate family.

Midlife Crisis: Reshaping Emotional Portfolios

The term "midlife crisis" is often misunderstood. Rather than being a superficial pursuit of youth, it represents a deeper reckoning with unmet needs and unresolved dreams. This phase prompts individuals to audit their emotional portfolio and recalibrate their investments in alignment with their values.

The Catalyst for Change

A midlife crisis often begins with a sense of dissatisfaction or longing. This feeling, while uncomfortable, serves as a signal that growth is needed.

For example, someone who prioritized external validation may feel unfulfilled despite their achievements. Another individual might yearn for creative expression after years of neglecting personal passions. These realizations, though painful, provide a foundation for transformation.

Reshaping Emotional Investments

Reshaping an emotional portfolio involves redistributing time and energy toward what truly matters. This might mean reconnecting with neglected relationships, pursuing hobbies, or embracing new challenges. It also requires letting go of unfulfilling commitments, freeing emotional resources for meaningful pursuits.

Midlife crises often lead to profound growth. By confronting fears, desires, and regrets, individuals emerge with a renewed sense of purpose and authenticity.

Tracing the Patterns

The patterns that emerge during midlife often reflect unresolved issues from earlier stages of life. Career choices, relationship dynamics, and parenting styles carry echoes of childhood and adolescence, revealing the interconnectedness of our emotional journeys.

Breaking the Cycle

Breaking free from unhelpful patterns requires self- awareness and intentionality. For example, a person who habitually prioritizes others' needs over their own might learn to set boundaries. Similarly, someone who avoids vulnerability may develop the courage to embrace deeper connections.

By revisiting past experiences with honesty, individuals gain the clarity needed to make intentional changes. This process is not about erasing the past but about integrating its lessons into a more balanced and fulfilling present.

Revisiting Midlife Accounts

Midlife is a time of profound change and opportunity. It invites individuals to audit their emotional ledger, reconciling past choices with present realities while envisioning future possibilities.

This stage is not just about reckoning with what has been lost or left undone; it is about rediscovering what truly matters. By embracing the lessons of midlife, individuals can move forward with a renewed sense of purpose, building a legacy of emotional wealth that enriches their lives and those of others.

Moving Forward

Midlife reckoning is both a challenge and an opportunity. It offers a chance to confront unresolved issues, recalibrate priorities, and invest in emotional prosperity. The experiences of this stage— career transitions, relationship dynamics, parenting challenges, and existential crises—are not merely obstacles; they are gateways to growth and fulfillment.

As we continue this journey, the next chapter will explore the golden years, where the lessons of midlife come to fruition. In embracing change and reflection, individuals can create a future rich in connection, resilience, and meaning.

CHAPTER 5

The Golden Years & Legacy Emotional Estate Planning

The golden years symbolize both a culmination and a new beginning. With the frenetic pace of earlier decades behind us, this phase invites reflection, renewal, and reinvention. As careers wind down and families grow, the emotional ledger undergoes one final audit. Retirement, grandparenting, and encounters with loss bring opportunities for growth and connection, while the life review process invites us to balance emotional accounts and shape a lasting legacy.

This chapter explores four pivotal aspects of the golden years: retirement as a rebalancing of emotional investments, grandparenting as an act of intergenerational generosity, coping with grief as a path to closure, and the final tallying of life's emotional ledger as a framework for legacy-building.

Retirement: Rebalancing Emotional Investments

Retirement often marks a significant shift in identity and purpose. It represents both an end and a beginning, offering time for introspection, new pursuits, and deeper connections. Yet, this transition requires a recalibration of emotional priorities and investments.

Letting Go of Old Roles

For decades, careers often define a significant part of our identity. Retirement dissolves those structures, leaving a blank slate that can feel liberating for some and disorienting for others. Without the daily rhythm of work, individuals may grapple with questions like, "Who am I without my career?" and "What do I contribute now?"

These questions highlight the need to reconcile unresolved emotional debts tied to professional life. A person who sacrificed family time for career advancement may feel regret, while another might struggle to let go of the validation tied to their professional success. Acknowledging these feelings allows individuals to focus on the possibilities ahead rather than the roles left behind.

Exploring New Horizons

Retirement opens doors to long-neglected passions, hobbies, and relationships. Activities like volunteering, traveling, or learning new skills not only bring joy but also deposit purpose and connection into the emotional ledger.

This phase is also an opportunity for personal growth. Many retirees turn inward, exploring spirituality or addressing unresolved emotional patterns. By dedicating time to reflection and intentional living, they cultivate a deeper sense of fulfillment.

Grandparenting: Generational Emotional Transfers

Grandparenting offers a unique opportunity to create lasting emotional wealth. Free from the daily responsibilities of parenting, grandparents can focus on nurturing and connecting with their grandchildren in meaningful ways.

A Second Chance at Connection

For many, grandparenting feels like a second chance to nurture. Mistakes made during parenting—such as impatience or overemphasis on discipline—can be revisited and reframed through this new role.

Grandparents often find joy in unhurried moments with their grandchildren, fostering bonds that enrich both lives.

This dynamic is mutually beneficial. Grandchildren gain unconditional love and wisdom, while grandparents experience the fulfillment of giving without expectation. These moments become deposits in an intergenerational emotional ledger, creating ripples that extend far beyond the present.

Passing Down Emotional Wealth

Grandparents play a critical role in shaping family narratives and values. Through stories, traditions, and lessons, they pass down emotional wealth that influences future generations.

For instance, sharing stories of perseverance during challenging times instills resilience, while modeling empathy and gratitude provides a template for healthy relationships. These contributions form an intangible but enduring legacy, enriching the family's emotional economy.

Coping with Grief and Loss

The golden years often bring encounters with loss— whether through the passing of loved ones, changes in physical health, or the end of long-held dreams. These losses, though painful, also present opportunities for growth and transformation.

Acknowledging the Pain

Grief is an unavoidable part of life's later stages. The loss of a spouse, sibling, or close friend leaves a profound void, unearthing layers of unresolved emotions. Suppressing grief only deepens emotional debts; while acknowledging it allows for healing.

For many, grief acts as a mirror, reflecting past experiences of loss. The death of a loved one might rekindle memories of earlier separations, such as childhood abandonment or relationship breakdowns. Confronting these emotions, though difficult, fosters emotional integration and closure.

Finding Meaning in Loss

Grief also clarifies priorities, highlighting what truly matters in life. While loss often feels overwhelming, it deepens our capacity for connection and empathy.

Through rituals, support networks, or personal reflection, individuals can transform grief into a source of meaning. These processes not only heal but also strengthen the foundation for legacy-building, ensuring that the lessons learned from loss inspire others.

Final Balances: A Life Reviewed

As individuals approach the later years of life, they often feel compelled to review their emotional ledger. This process is not about achieving perfection but about finding coherence and meaning in the story of one's life.

Revisiting the Past

A life review often involves revisiting key moments—both triumphs and regrets—and examining how they have shaped the journey. This reflection celebrates relationships that enriched life while seeking closure on those that caused pain or remained unresolved.

For instance, reaching out to estranged family members or expressing forgiveness can bring profound relief. Writing letters, even if unsent, can provide a way to articulate gratitude or seek closure. These acts reconcile the past, balancing the emotional ledger with integrity.

Building a Legacy

Legacy is about more than material wealth—it is the emotional and relational imprints we leave behind. By prioritizing relationships, practicing forgiveness, and sharing wisdom, individuals create ripples that extend beyond their own lives.

For example, mentoring younger generations passes down emotional wealth in the form of encouragement and example.

These contributions enrich the lives of others, becoming a cornerstone of legacy-building.

Tracing the Imprints

The golden years are a culmination of the patterns established throughout life. Yet, they also offer the greatest opportunity for transformation and healing.

Healing the Wounds

Unresolved issues often resurface in this stage, particularly within family dynamics or old friendships. Confronting these patterns with honesty and compassion allows individuals to break cycles and foster peace.

For instance, reconciling with an estranged child or sibling, even after years of silence, can deposit immense value into the emotional ledger. These acts redefine the narrative, leaving behind a legacy of connection rather than division.

Moving Forward

The golden years are not just about endings; they are about beginnings. They offer a chance to revisit the emotional ledger with fresh eyes, celebrating gains, making peace with losses, and embracing new opportunities for growth and connection.

By approaching this stage with intention and reflection, individuals can balance the books of their lives, leaving behind a legacy rooted in love, wisdom, and generosity. As we transition into the next phase of this journey, the focus shifts toward strategies for reconciliation and healing, providing tools to continue cultivating emotional prosperity.

CHAPTER 6

Identifying Emotional Creditors & Debtors

Reconciliation begins with awareness. The relationships that define our lives are shaped by emotional transactions, both enriching and depleting. Every bond—whether enduring or fleeting—leaves entries in our emotional ledger. To move forward, we must identify the "creditors" who have poured into us, the "debtors" who have drained us, and the patterns of exchange that define our connections.

This chapter focuses on the essential steps of mapping emotional networks, understanding relational dynamics, uncovering hidden emotional costs, and evaluating the true value of our emotional assets. Together, these steps offer clarity on how to achieve balance and purpose in relationships.

Emotional Ties: Mapping Networks

Our emotional networks represent the web of relationships that connect us to others. Each thread tells a story of shared experiences, acts of kindness, misunderstandings, or unmet needs. Mapping these networks allows us to identify the contributors to our emotional well-being and those who challenge it.

Identifying Key Connections

Start by identifying the most significant relationships in your life—family, friends, mentors, colleagues, and romantic partners. For each, reflect on their role in your emotional ledger. Did they deposit love, trust, or guidance? Or did they withdraw through neglect, criticism, or unmet expectations?

Consider relationships that span years and those that were brief yet impactful. For instance, a teacher's encouragement during a pivotal moment might have shaped your confidence, while a fleeting friendship may have left a lasting impression of betrayal.

Recognizing Relational Impact

Mapping your network helps reveal the balance of emotional exchanges. Some bonds may feel enriching, fostering growth and joy. Others might weigh heavily, creating tension or unease. This exercise is not about assigning blame but about gaining clarity on how these connections shape your emotional landscape.

Patterns in Emotional Giving and Taking

Healthy relationships thrive on reciprocity, but imbalances often emerge. Some people give selflessly, while others take without replenishing. Recognizing these patterns offers valuable insight into relational dynamics.

The Over-Giver

Over-givers prioritize others' needs over their own, often equating love with sacrifice. While their generosity strengthens bonds, it can also lead to exhaustion and resentment. This behavior often stems from early experiences where affection was conditional on meeting expectations.

To break this pattern, over-givers must learn to set boundaries and practice self-care. Ask: *Am I giving out of genuine desire, or am I seeking validation?*

The Over-Taker

Over-takers rely heavily on others, often without realizing the imbalance. This tendency may stem from a fear of scarcity— believing their needs will go unmet unless they take from others.

Recognizing this behavior requires humility. Over-takers should ask: *Am I giving as much as I take? How can I restore balance in my relationships?*

Balancing the Scales

Most relationships fall somewhere between over-giving and over-taking. Striving for balance involves honest communication, clear boundaries, and mutual respect. By fostering equity, relationships become sustainable and enriching for both parties.

Unseen Costs of Emotional Deficits

Not all emotional debts are immediately visible. Some linger beneath the surface, accruing interest until they demand attention. Identifying these hidden costs is essential for reconciliation.

The Burden of Unspoken Grievances

Unaddressed hurts—whether a partner's dismissive comment or a friend's betrayal—create lingering emotional deficits. Over time, these unresolved grievances erode trust and intimacy, leaving relationships strained or fractured.

Acknowledging these grievances involves naming the hurt and reflecting on its impact. Ask: *How has this experience shaped my behavior or perceptions? What steps can I take to address it constructively?*

The Ripple Effect of Neglect

Unmet emotional needs often ripple outward, affecting other areas of life. A child neglected by a parent may struggle with attachment in adulthood, while someone undervalued at work might carry frustration into personal relationships.

Understanding these ripples helps individuals take ownership of their emotional patterns and begin the work of healing and prevention.

Recognizing Patterns of Give and Take

By examining relational dynamics, we uncover patterns of giving, receiving, and withholding. These patterns often originate in early experiences and influence present behaviors.

Relational Imbalances

Some relationships thrive on mutual support, while others are marked by imbalance. For example, a friend who consistently leans on you for emotional support without reciprocating may leave you feeling drained. Conversely, a relationship where you rarely give back can lead to guilt or disconnection.

The Impact of Context

Context matters. During stressful periods, such as a loved one's illness or a career transition, temporary imbalances are natural. Recognizing when these dynamics become long-term or toxic is crucial for maintaining emotional health.

Assessing the Value of Emotional Assets

While deficits weigh on our emotional ledger, assets provide strength and resilience. These assets—relationships, experiences, and personal qualities—are the foundation of emotional prosperity.

Valuing Positive Contributions

Acts of kindness, encouragement, and love leave lasting imprints. Reflect on the people who have added value to your life. Who celebrated your victories? Who offered a listening ear during challenges?

These positive contributions are often overlooked but deserve recognition. Acknowledging them reinforces gratitude and strengthens bonds.

Recognizing Internal Strengths

Emotional assets are not limited to external relationships. Qualities like empathy, resilience, and self-awareness enrich our interactions and foster personal growth. Reflecting on how you have cultivated these strengths deepens your understanding of your emotional wealth.

The Hidden Toll of Emotional Deficits

While assets enrich us, deficits demand attention.

Emotional debts—unresolved guilt, lingering resentment, or unmet needs—drain our reserves and prevent us from thriving.

Uncovering Buried Debts

Reflect on relationships that bring discomfort or unease. Are there unresolved tensions or unspoken regrets? What debts— apologies, forgiveness, gratitude—remain unpaid?

By identifying these debts, you take the first step toward reconciliation.

Measuring Emotional Assets Accurately

Balancing emotional accounts requires a clear understanding of your assets and liabilities. By evaluating both tangible and intangible contributions, you can prioritize relationships that align with your values.

Short-Term and Long-Term Impacts

Some relationships offer immediate gratification, while others yield long-term benefits. For example, caring for an aging parent may feel emotionally taxing in the moment but fosters deep connection and purpose over time.

Conversely, relationships that seem enjoyable but lack depth may offer little lasting value. Reflect on which connections enrich your life and which may need re-evaluation.

Tracing the Imprints

Mapping your emotional network often reveals deeper patterns rooted in childhood, adolescence, or past relationships. Understanding these origins provides context for current behaviors and dynamics.

Revisiting Early Influences

Family dynamics, early friendships, and formative experiences shape our emotional patterns. A parent's criticism, a sibling's rivalry, or a peer's betrayal leaves imprints that influence how we connect with others.

Revisiting these influences with compassion—not blame— allows for growth and healing. By recognizing the roots of your patterns, you gain clarity on how to break cycles and foster healthier relationships.

Owning Your Role

True reconciliation requires taking responsibility for your part in relational imbalances. Reflect on instances where you may have fallen short—whether by withholding gratitude, avoiding conflict, or failing to reciprocate support.

Owning your role fosters humility and paves the way for genuine connection.

Moving Forward

Identifying emotional creditors and debtors is not an end but a beginning. By mapping your network, recognizing patterns, and assessing assets, you lay the groundwork for reconciliation and healing. This process enriches your emotional ledger, fostering relationships built on mutual investment and trust.

As we continue this journey, the focus shifts to actionable strategies for paying emotional debts and restoring harmony in our connections. Each step brings us closer to a life defined by balance, purpose, and emotional prosperity.

CHAPTER 7

Strategies for Emotional Debt Repayment

Reconciliation requires action. Emotional debts, whether created by neglect, misunderstanding, or harm, cannot remain unresolved indefinitely. To truly move forward, we must confront these debts—both those we owe and those owed to us. Emotional healing involves genuine apologies, the power of forgiveness, the act of restitution, and the courage to extend compassion to ourselves.

This chapter explores the tangible steps toward emotional debt repayment: mastering the art of sincere apologies, embracing forgiveness as liberation, restoring bonds through deliberate actions, and practicing self-forgiveness to achieve inner peace.

The Art of a Sincere Apology

A sincere apology is the cornerstone of emotional reconciliation. More than mere words, it is a demonstration of accountability and a commitment to repair. However, apologies that lack depth—those offered from obligation or discomfort— often do more harm than good.

The Anatomy of a Genuine Apology

A true apology comprises three essential elements: acknowledgment, ownership, and commitment.

1. **Acknowledgment:** Begin by identifying the specific harm caused. Avoid vague generalities like, "I'm sorry for everything." Instead, name the behavior and its impact: *I realize my harsh words during our argument made you feel unappreciated and dismissed.*

2. **Ownership:** Accept full responsibility for your actions without deflecting blame or diluting the apology. Avoid phrases like, *"I didn't mean to hurt you"* or *"I was under a lot of stress."* These explanations shift the focus from the injured party to the offender. Instead, focus on accountability: *"What I did was wrong, and I deeply regret it."*
3. **Commitment:** A genuine apology is forward-looking, offering a path to rebuild trust: *"I'm committed to being more mindful of my words and listening to you without interrupting."*

The Importance of Timing and Intention

An apology should not be rushed or delivered when emotions are high. Take time to reflect on the harm caused and approach the conversation with humility. The goal is not to alleviate your guilt but to validate the other person's experience and begin the process of repair.

Forgiveness: Writing Off Emotional Debts

If apologies are about paying debts owed, forgiveness is about letting go of debts owed to us. Forgiveness does not mean condoning harmful behavior or forgetting the pain endured; it is an act of liberation, a decision to free oneself from the grip of resentment.

Understanding the Nature of Forgiveness

Forgiveness is often misunderstood as weakness or acquiescence. In reality, it is an act of strength. It shifts the focus from the offender to your own healing, allowing you to reclaim emotional energy tied up in anger and hurt.

Holding onto resentment may feel protective, but it often backfires. Bitterness becomes a heavy burden, clouding judgment and limiting emotional freedom. Forgiveness clears this weight, enabling you to invest in relationships and experiences that nourish you.

The Process of Forgiving Others

Forgiveness is not instantaneous; it unfolds in stages:
1. **Acknowledge the Pain:** Validate your feelings of hurt without minimizing them. Identify what was taken from you—trust, respect, or a sense of safety—and allow yourself to grieve those losses.
2. **Reframe the Narrative:** Empathy is a powerful tool for forgiveness. While not excusing harmful actions, understanding the offender's perspective can soften resentment. For example, recognizing a parent's emotional unavailability as a result of their struggles may make it easier to let go of anger.
3. **Release the Hold:** Forgiveness is a decision to release the emotional tether that ties you to the offender. It does not always require reconciliation but focuses on creating peace within yourself.

Restitution: Repairing Through Action

While apologies are essential, words alone may not suffice for deep wounds. Restitution—taking tangible steps to repair the harm—demonstrates sincerity and fosters trust.

Restoring Balance Through Actions

Restitution involves recognizing the specific needs of the injured party and addressing them with intention. Examples include:
- Rebuilding trust in a damaged partnership through consistent, transparent communication.
- Showing up for a friend you have neglected by prioritizing quality time together.

- Offering acts of service to atone for past selfishness, such as supporting a sibling during a challenging time.

These actions, though sometimes small, carry significant emotional weight. They signal your willingness to invest in the relationship's healing and growth.

Patience and Persistence

Restitution requires time. Emotional debts often accrue over years and cannot be resolved overnight. Be patient with the process, recognizing that meaningful change involves sustained effort and consistency.

Self-Forgiveness: Settling Debts with Yourself

We are often harsher on ourselves than we are on others, carrying guilt and shame for years. Self-forgiveness is the act of releasing self-blame and embracing self-compassion.

Acknowledging Personal Imperfections

Self-forgiveness begins with acknowledgment. Recognize where you have fallen short—whether in your relationships, decisions, or self-care. This acknowledgment must be honest yet compassionate. Instead of dwelling on past mistakes, frame them as opportunities for growth: *"I made choices that hurt myself and others, but I've learned from them."*

Making Amends to Yourself

Just as you would apologize to a friend, extend the same kindness to yourself. Identify areas where you have neglected your own needs or acted against your values and commit to change. For instance, if you have prioritized work over health, begin setting boundaries to create balance.

Letting Go of Perfectionism

Self-forgiveness involves embracing imperfection.

Mistakes do not define your worth; they are part of the human experience. By accepting this, you free yourself from the paralyzing effects of guilt and focus on moving forward with intention.

The Role of Vulnerability in Reconciliation

Reconciliation—whether with others or yourself—requires vulnerability. It demands openness, honesty, and a willingness to confront discomfort. While vulnerability may feel risky, it is the foundation for authentic connection and healing.

Creating Safe Spaces for Vulnerability

Approach conversations about reconciliation with care.

Ensure the environment is conducive to honest dialogue, free from judgment or defensiveness. This fosters trust and encourages both parties to share openly.

Practicing Vulnerability with Yourself

Being vulnerable with yourself means confronting difficult truths without avoidance. Reflect on your emotional debts and credits with honesty, recognizing both your strengths and areas for improvement.

Moving Forward: A Blueprint for Emotional Healing

Emotional debt repayment is an ongoing process that requires commitment and adaptability. Some relationships will flourish with time and effort; others may remain strained despite your best intentions. The goal is not perfection but progress-small incremental steps that lead to great emotional balance and fulfilment.

Questions for Reflection and Action

- *What apologies do I need to offer, and to whom?*
- *What relationships require acts of restitution to restore trust?*
- *What emotional debts am I holding onto that I can release through forgiveness?*
- *How can I practice greater self-compassion moving forward?*

By reflecting on these questions and taking deliberate action, you can transform unresolved debts into opportunities for growth and connection.

Conclusion: The Power of Reconciliation

Paying emotional debts is a courageous act of accountability and healing. Whether through apologies, forgiveness, restitution, or self-compassion, each step strengthens your emotional ledger and enriches your relationships.

As we move into the next chapter, the focus will shift to rebuilding emotional prosperity—cultivating habits and relationships that foster long-term fulfillment and resilience. Each act of reconciliation is a building block for a life defined by balance, connection, and growth.

CHAPTER 8

Healing Emotional Bankruptcy

Recognizing Signs of Emotional Insolvency

Emotional bankruptcy is a state of profound depletion—a place where the demands on your emotional reserves outstrip your ability to replenish them. Like financial insolvency, it does not occur overnight but builds gradually through prolonged neglect, unresolved pain, or unbalanced relationships.

The Early Warning Signs

Emotional insolvency manifests in subtle ways at first.
These signs often intensify if left unaddressed:
1. **Chronic Fatigue**: No amount of rest seems to restore your energy.
2. **Emotional Numbness**: Joy, sadness, and excitement feel distant or muted.
3. **Irritability**: Minor inconveniences provoke outsize reactions.
4. **Withdrawal**: Relationships feel draining, prompting isolation.
5. **Loss of Purpose**: Life feels directionless, as though meaning has been siphoned away.

Tracing the Causes

Emotional bankruptcy stems from patterns and circumstances that deplete rather than sustain. Common culprits include:
- Overextending yourself in caregiving roles.
- Neglecting self-care to meet external obligations.
- Carrying unresolved grief, trauma, or guilt.
- Enduring toxic or one-sided relationships.

Recognizing these causes is an essential first step toward recovery, enabling you to confront the roots of your emotional depletion with clarity and courage.

Emotional Chapter II: Restructuring Your Feelings

Just as a financially struggling business must restructure to survive, individuals experiencing emotional bankruptcy must reassess their priorities to restore balance. Pushing through without addressing the root causes only deepens the deficit.

Setting Boundaries

Boundaries are essential for preserving emotional resources. Begin with small steps, such as:

- Saying no to commitments that feel overwhelming.
- Reducing interactions with those who consistently drain you.
- Prioritizing personal time without guilt.

Boundaries are not barriers; they are tools for maintaining healthy connections while protecting your well-being.

Reevaluating Emotional Investments

Examine your relationships and activities through the lens of nourishment versus depletion:

- Which relationships bring joy, support, and growth?
- Which leave you feeling drained or unappreciated?

Shift your focus toward those that replenish your emotional reserves, even if it means letting go of those that do not.

Processing Unresolved Emotions

Unacknowledged feelings—whether grief, anger, or shame—quietly erode your emotional foundation. Address these emotions through journaling, meditation, or therapy. Release what no longer serves you and create space for healing.

Restructuring your emotional framework is not about erasing the past but building a sustainable path forward—one where your energy is spent in alignment with your values.

A Plan for Emotional Recovery

Healing from emotional bankruptcy requires intentional action. A structured plan provides a roadmap for replenishing emotional reserves and regaining balance.

Step 1: Rest and Replenish

Rest is foundational. Prioritize restorative activities, such as:
- Consistent, quality sleep.
- Gentle movements like yoga or walking.
- Time spent in nature, which calms the nervous system.

Rest is not indulgence—it is a necessary investment in your recovery.

Step 2: Set Firm Boundaries

Identify areas where overextension has left you depleted.
Protect your time and energy by:
- Limiting obligations that do not align with your priorities.
- Creating clear expectations in relationships.
- Practicing saying no with confidence.

Step 3: Reconnect with Joy

Rediscover activities that bring happiness. Pursue hobbies, explore creative outlets, or engage in experiences that ignite passion and curiosity. These moments deposit energy into your emotional ledger.

Step 4: Seek Support

Recovery is not a solitary journey. Turn to trusted friends, family, or support groups who can provide encouragement and perspective.

Building Emotional Self-Worth

Rebuilding self-worth is central to emotional recovery. When you value yourself, you are less likely to overextend or tolerate harmful dynamics.

Celebrate Small Wins

Acknowledge even modest progress—setting a boundary, prioritizing rest, or taking steps toward healing. These victories reinforce a sense of capability and confidence.

Practice Daily Affirmations

Positive affirmations reshape your inner dialogue. Remind yourself:
- "I am worthy of love and respect."
- "My needs are valid."
- "I am growing stronger each day."

Cultivate Gratitude for Yourself

Reflect on moments of resilience, growth, and kindness you have shown. By focusing on these strengths, you reinforce your inherent value.

Building an Emergency Fund of Self-Compassion

Self-compassion acts as a reserve of inner strength during difficult times. To cultivate self-compassion:

- Replace self-criticism with supportive language: *"It is okay to feel this way. I am doing my best."*
- Acknowledge the shared humanity of struggle: Suffering connects us, reminding us we are not alone.
- Practice mindfulness to observe emotions without judgment, creating space for healing.

Seeking Professional Help: Emotional Advisors

Just as financial advisors guide individuals through economic challenges, therapists and counselors offer invaluable support during emotional insolvency.

The Role of Therapy

Therapy provides a safe space to explore unresolved emotions, identify destructive patterns, and develop strategies for recovery. Therapists act as guides, offering tools to navigate emotional struggles with clarity and resilience.

Choosing the Right Therapist

Find a therapist whose expertise aligns with your needs.

Whether addressing trauma, relationship dynamics, or stress, select someone who fosters trust and understanding.

Therapeutic Techniques

Effective therapy often incorporates:

- **Mindfulness:** Cultivating presence and reducing stress.

- **Cognitive Restructuring:** Challenging limiting beliefs.
- **Narrative Therapy:** Rewriting personal stories to emphasize growth.

Breaking the Cycle of Emotional Bankruptcy

Recovery requires breaking patterns that led to depletion.
This may involve:

- Leaving toxic relationships.
- Reevaluating career choices that prioritize productivity over well-being.
- Challenging societal expectations that glorify overextension.

Breaking these cycles creates space for a life aligned with your emotional needs.

Investing in Emotional Wealth

True recovery is not just about replenishment but also about building emotional abundance. This involves:

- **Prioritizing Rest:** Make rest a daily habit, not a rare indulgence.
- **Nurturing Relationships:** Invest in connections that uplift and support.
- **Practicing Gratitude:** Focus on what enriches your life, reinforcing positivity.

Moving Forward: Reclaiming Balance

Healing from emotional bankruptcy is a courageous act of self-love. It requires persistence, reflection, and a commitment to prioritizing your well-being. As you take these steps, remember:

1. Recovery is a journey, not a race.
2. Setbacks are natural and do not erase progress.
3. Every small step toward balance is a victory.

As we transition to the next chapter, we will explore how to build emotional wealth and ensure lasting growth. By addressing emotional bankruptcy with intention and resilience, you create a foundation for a life of joy, connection, and abundance.

CHAPTER 9

Building Emotional Wealth
Investing in Emotional Capital

The Foundation of Emotional Wealth

Emotional wealth is the cornerstone of meaningful relationships and personal fulfillment. Unlike material wealth, it multiplies through sharing and deepens over time. Cultivating emotional wealth requires intentionality, courage, and consistent effort, but its rewards are immeasurable: stronger connections, greater resilience, and a life rooted in purpose.

This chapter explores four key pillars of emotional wealth: cultivating empathy, embracing vulnerability, building trust, and practicing gratitude. Each of these elements contributes to an emotional ledger that grows richer with time, enhancing both individual well-being and collective harmony.

Cultivating Empathy: The Gold Standard of Emotional Capital

Empathy is the ability to deeply understand and share the feelings of another. It is the gold standard of emotional capital, enriching relationships by fostering understanding, connection, and compassion.

Perspective-Taking

Empathy begins with seeing the world through another's eyes. This involves setting aside assumptions and judgments to truly understand their experience. For instance, instead of dismissing a friend's anxiety about a job interview, consider the pressures they may feel to succeed.

Perspective-taking does not require agreement; it requires acknowledgment. Simple phrases like "I can see why this feels overwhelming for you" validate others' emotions and build bridges of connection.

Active Listening

Active listening transforms empathy into action. It involves giving undivided attention, asking thoughtful questions, and reflecting back what you hear. This practice strengthens relationships by demonstrating genuine care.

During a disagreement, for example, saying, "Tell me more about how this is affecting you," shifts the focus from winning an argument to understanding and resolution.

Overcoming Barriers to Empathy

Common barriers to empathy include distraction, judgment, and self-centered thinking. Cultivating empathy requires mindfulness—being present in the moment and attuned to others' emotions. It also involves challenging biases and remaining open to perspectives different from your own.

Vulnerability: High-Risk, High-Reward Emotional Investing

Vulnerability is often misunderstood as a weakness, but it is, in fact, a profound strength. It is the willingness to expose your true self—fears, dreams, and insecurities—in pursuit of deeper connection and authenticity.

The Courage to Be Vulnerable

Being vulnerable requires courage. It means risking rejection or judgment to foster genuine intimacy. For instance, sharing a personal struggle with a friend might feel risky but often leads to mutual support and understanding.

Vulnerability is not about oversharing; it is about intentional openness. Gradually revealing more of yourself as trust deepens ensures that vulnerability strengthens relationships rather than overwhelming them.

Building Emotional Intimacy

Vulnerability paves the way for emotional intimacy. By sharing your inner world, you create a space where others feel safe to do the same. This mutual exchange enriches emotional reserves, creating bonds that are both authentic and enduring.

Balancing Vulnerability with Boundaries

While vulnerability is essential, it must be balanced with boundaries. Not every relationship warrants full transparency.

Learn to gauge when and with whom vulnerability is appropriate, ensuring that it enhances rather than strains your connections.

Trust: A Critical Emotional Asset

Trust is the foundation of emotional wealth. It is the assurance that someone is reliable, honest, and committed to your well-being. Without trust, relationships falter; with it, they thrive.

Building Trust Through Consistency

Trust is built through small, consistent actions. Showing up when you say you will, following through on promises, and being honest even in uncomfortable moments demonstrate reliability.

Over time, these behaviors establish a foundation of trust.

Repairing Broken Trust

When trust is broken, repair is possible but requires effort and accountability. Start by acknowledging the breach without deflecting blame. Commit to actions that rebuild confidence, such as being transparent and dependable over time.

For example, if a broken promise caused harm, ensure that future commitments are honored without fail. Trust grows when others see genuine effort and change.

Trusting Yourself

Trust is not limited to others; it also involves trusting yourself. This means honoring your own boundaries, values, and instincts. When you trust yourself, you are less likely to tolerate disrespect or compromise your well-being for the sake of others.

Gratitude: Compound Interest for the Soul

Gratitude is a transformative practice that amplifies emotional wealth. It shifts focus from what is lacking to what is present, fostering positivity and deepening connections.

Practicing Mindful Gratitude

Gratitude begins with mindfulness—paying attention to life's small blessings. Whether it is the warmth of the sun on your face or a kind word from a friend, these moments of appreciation cultivate a mindset of abundance.

Expressing Gratitude to Others

Expressing gratitude strengthens relationships by acknowledging their impact. Instead of a generic "Thanks," opt for specific and heartfelt acknowledgments, like, "I really appreciate how you supported me during that tough conversation."

Small gestures—a handwritten note, a sincere compliment, or a simple thank-you—reinforce emotional bonds and demonstrate care.

Practicing Gratitude During Challenges

Gratitude is especially powerful in adversity. It reframes struggles by highlighting sources of support and resilience. For instance, during a difficult period, reflecting on the kindness of friends or the lessons learned fosters hope and perspective.

Investing in Emotional Capital

Building emotional wealth involves intentional investments in habits and relationships that nurture growth and resilience.

Breaking Old Patterns

To foster emotional abundance, it is essential to break patterns rooted in scarcity or fear. This might mean letting go of defensive behaviors, addressing unresolved pain, or challenging beliefs that hinder vulnerability and trust.

Prioritizing Meaningful Connections

Invest time and energy in relationships that uplift and inspire you. Acts of kindness, shared experiences, and honest communication strengthen bonds and add deposits to your emotional ledger.

Creating Daily Practices

Incorporate habits that cultivate emotional wealth into your daily life. This might include:

- Journaling about moments of joy and gratitude.

- Engaging in acts of kindness, such as volunteering or helping a neighbor.
- Practicing mindfulness to remain present and attuned to your emotions.

Tracing the Path to Emotional Prosperity

Building emotional wealth is not a one-time effort but a lifelong practice. Each act of empathy, vulnerability, trust, and gratitude contributes to a richer and more fulfilling emotional ledger.

Revisiting Emotional Investments

Regularly reflect on your emotional investments. Are your relationships and habits contributing to your growth? If not, consider making adjustments that align with your values and goals.

Creating a Ripple Effect

Emotional wealth does not just benefit you—it enriches your community. By embodying empathy, vulnerability, trust, and gratitude, you inspire others to do the same, creating a ripple effect of connection and compassion.

Moving Forward

Emotional wealth is an invaluable resource, offering a foundation for deeper relationships, greater resilience, and lasting fulfillment. By investing in empathy, embracing vulnerability, fostering trust, and practicing gratitude, you cultivate a reservoir of emotional resources that sustains and uplifts both yourself and those around you.

As we move into the next chapter, we will explore how to sustain these practices over the long term, ensuring that your emotional wealth continues to grow and enrich your life.

CHAPTER 10

Navigating Emotional Mergers & Acquisitions

The Complexities of Emotional Mergers

Relationships often involve merging emotional worlds.

Whether blending families, navigating workplace dynamics, bridging cultural divides, or managing digital connections, these "emotional mergers and acquisitions" require deliberate effort. Successfully integrating multiple emotional ecosystems involves balancing respect, communication, and adaptability while addressing past emotional debts.

This chapter explores four key domains of emotional mergers—blended families, workplace dynamics, cultural integration, and virtual connections—offering strategies to navigate these complexities while fostering connection and growth.

Blended Families: Combining Emotional Assets

Blending families is one of the most intricate emotional mergers, bringing together individuals with diverse histories, values, and needs. This process requires patience, communication, and a commitment to creating a shared emotional framework.

Acknowledging Emotional Luggage

Every member of a blended family brings emotional "luggage"—past experiences, loyalties, and fears. A child may struggle with the memory of a previous family dynamic, while a stepparent might navigate feelings of inadequacy or rejection.

Recognizing and validating these emotions is the first step toward building trust.

For example, a child hesitant to accept a stepparent might need time and reassurance that their feelings are understood and respected. Open conversations about past experiences and current concerns help ease these transitions.

Creating Shared Traditions

Blended families thrive when they build new traditions that reflect their unique identity. These rituals foster unity and create opportunities for emotional bonding. For instance, a weekly game night or a holiday tradition can help strengthen connections and establish a sense of belonging.

Balancing Individual Needs with Collective Harmony

In a blended family, respecting individual boundaries is as important as fostering collective harmony. Not every relationship will develop at the same pace, and that is okay. Allow relationships to evolve naturally without imposing expectations of immediate closeness.

Workplace Dynamics: Emotional Accounting in Professional Relationships

The workplace is a significant arena for emotional transactions. Navigating workplace dynamics requires balancing personal ambition with collective goals, fostering trust, and managing conflict constructively.

Cultivating Emotional Intelligence at Work

Emotional intelligence—awareness of one's emotions and those of others—is essential for navigating workplace dynamics. A manager's ability to empathize with their team, for example, can foster loyalty and motivation. Similarly, employees who practice self-awareness and empathy contribute to a collaborative environment.

Balancing Ambition and Collaboration

While striving for individual success, it is crucial to remain mindful of team dynamics. Overemphasizing personal achievements at the expense of collaboration can strain relationships. Conversely, neglecting personal goals may lead to frustration. Striking this balance involves clear communication about expectations and contributions.

Constructive Conflict Resolution

Conflict is inevitable in professional settings, but it does not have to be destructive. Approach disagreements with curiosity rather than defensiveness. For example, instead of blaming a colleague during a disagreement, focus on understanding their perspective and finding common ground.

Recognizing and Rewarding Effort

Acknowledgment is a powerful deposit in the emotional ledger of workplace relationships. Simple acts like expressing gratitude for a colleague's effort or celebrating team milestones create a positive environment and strengthen professional bonds.

Cultural Integration: Bridging Emotional Exchange Rates

In an increasingly interconnected world, cross-cultural relationships are becoming more common. Navigating these dynamics requires curiosity, respect, and adaptability.

Understanding Emotional Currencies

Different cultures express emotions, resolve conflicts, and build trust in unique ways. For example, some cultures value direct communication, while others prioritize subtlety to preserve harmony. Recognizing and adapting to these differences prevents misunderstandings and fosters connection.

Celebrating Diversity and Shared Values

While cultural differences may seem daunting, shared values often provide a foundation for connection. A couple from different cultural backgrounds, for instance, might bond over shared goals like raising compassionate children. By focusing on commonalities, individuals can bridge gaps and deepen relationships.

Avoiding Stereotypes

Assumptions based on stereotypes hinder cultural integration. Approach cross-cultural relationships with curiosity and an open mind. Ask thoughtful questions to understand the other person's perspective rather than relying on preconceived notions.

Digital Age Connections: Managing Virtual Emotional Portfolios

The digital age has transformed how we connect, offering opportunities for global relationships while introducing new challenges. Managing these virtual emotional portfolios requires intentionality and balance.

Authenticity in Digital Communication

Digital interactions often lack the nuance of face-to-face conversations. Prioritize clarity and authenticity to maintain meaningful connections. For instance, sending a heartfelt voice message or scheduling a video call can convey warmth and sincerity more effectively than text alone.

Overcoming Physical Distance

Virtual relationships, whether romantic, professional, or platonic, often face challenges of distance. Creative solutions— like watching movies together online or celebrating milestones virtually—help bridge these gaps and maintain emotional intimacy.

Balancing Online and Offline Engagement

While technology connects us, it can also overwhelm. Set boundaries to ensure screen time does not encroach on in-person relationships. For example, dedicate certain hours to being offline and fully present with loved ones.

Navigating Emotional Challenges

Emotional mergers and acquisitions often bring hidden challenges rooted in past experiences. Addressing these challenges requires reflection, communication, and a willingness to grow.

Breaking Old Patterns

Unresolved emotional debts from previous relationships can resurface in new dynamics, complicating integration. For example, a fear of rejection might lead someone to withdraw during conflicts. Identifying and addressing these patterns prevents them from sabotaging new relationships.

Embracing Growth Through Challenges

Each merger presents an opportunity for growth. By viewing challenges as learning experiences, individuals deepen their self-awareness and resilience while enriching their relationships.

Revisiting Emotional Mergers and Acquisitions

Navigating emotional mergers requires intention, patience, and adaptability. Whether blending families, fostering workplace connections, bridging cultural divides, or managing virtual bonds, each interaction is an opportunity to build emotional wealth.

The Role of Empathy and Respect

Empathy and respect are the cornerstones of successful mergers. By approaching every relationship with curiosity and care, individuals create environments where trust and connection thrive.

Continuing the Journey

Emotional mergers are not endpoints but part of an ongoing journey. Regularly revisiting and adjusting these dynamics ensures they remain sources of growth and fulfillment.

Moving Forward

Navigating emotional mergers and acquisitions is both a challenge and an opportunity. By blending families with care, fostering workplace harmony, bridging cultural differences, and managing digital connections, you create relationships that are dynamic, resilient, and enriching.

This chapter has offered strategies to approach these complexities with empathy and intentionality. As we continue this journey, the next chapter will explore emotional sustainability— ensuring the practices cultivated here endure as lasting sources of strength and connection.

CHAPTER 11

The Art of Emotional Budgeting

The Fundamentals of Emotional Budgeting

Emotions, like time or money, are finite resources. If mismanaged, they can be depleted, leaving individuals drained, unfulfilled, and unable to engage meaningfully in their lives.

Emotional budgeting is the practice of allocating emotional energy with care and intention, ensuring personal growth, nurturing relationships, and fostering long-term well-being.

This chapter explores strategies for spending emotional energy wisely, setting boundaries, prioritizing self-care, and fostering equality in relationships. Together, these practices create a balanced emotional framework that empowers individuals to thrive.

Allocating Emotional Resources Wisely

Effective emotional budgeting begins with prioritizing where your emotional energy goes. Just as financial planning involves assessing income and expenses, emotional budgeting requires clarity about what energizes you and what drains you.

Identifying Energy Drains

Certain relationships or commitments consume more emotional resources than they return. These may include one-sided friendships, unresolved conflicts, or situations where your efforts go unrecognized. For instance, a colleague who constantly demands help but never reciprocates may represent an emotional drain.

To manage this, evaluate the emotional return on investment (ROI) of your interactions. Ask yourself: Does this relationship or activity enrich me or exhaust me? Reducing energy spent on draining engagements creates room for more fulfilling pursuits.

Prioritizing Key Relationships

Not all connections require equal investment. Allocate more emotional energy to relationships that uplift and inspire you. For example, a close friend who listens without judgment or a partner who actively supports your goals deserves greater emotional focus than superficial or taxing acquaintances.

By prioritizing meaningful relationships, you ensure your emotional resources are spent where they yield the highest returns.

Adapting to Emotional Inflation

Over time, some commitments may demand more energy than they once did. A career that once excited you may now feel overwhelming, or a relationship that was energizing may become imbalanced. Recognizing these changes allows you to recalibrate your emotional investments.

Ask yourself: Am I allocating my emotional resources to reflect my values and goals? Adjust your focus as needed to align with your evolving priorities.

Setting Boundaries: Protecting Emotional Assets

Boundaries act as the guardrails of emotional budgeting, ensuring your resources are protected from overextension. They define your limits, allowing you to give authentically without compromising your well-being.

Recognizing Boundary Violations

Boundary violations often leave you feeling drained, resentful, or overwhelmed. For example, a friend who consistently disregards your time or a family member who intrudes on your personal space may signal the need for clearer boundaries.

Identifying these patterns is the first step toward reclaiming control over your emotional reserves.

Communicating Boundaries Effectively

Boundaries are only effective when communicated clearly and assertively. Use "I" statements to express your needs without assigning blame. For instance, say, "I need time to recharge after work before I can engage in conversation," rather than, "You're always overwhelming me."

Clear, respectful communication fosters understanding and reduces the likelihood of pushback.

Balancing Flexibility and Firmness

While boundaries should be firm, they must also allow for flexibility when appropriate. For example, accommodating a loved one's urgent needs may temporarily shift a boundary, but it should not become a permanent adjustment.

Balancing firmness with adaptability ensures your boundaries remain protective without becoming rigid.

Emotional Savings Plans: Investing in Self-Care

Building emotional resilience requires creating a "savings plan" through regular self-care. These reserves provide a buffer against life's challenges, enabling you to navigate stress, loss, or conflict without depleting your emotional energy.

Reclaiming Time for Yourself

Self-care begins with reclaiming time for activities that nourish your mind and spirit. These may include exercising, meditating, pursuing a creative hobby, or simply resting.

Even small, intentional acts—like a 10-minute walk or a mindful cup of tea—can restore emotional balance. The key is consistency. Treat self-care as a non-negotiable expense rather than a luxury.

Addressing Emotional Needs

Emotional self-care involves acknowledging and processing your feelings. Journaling, therapy, or confiding in a trusted friend provides an outlet for navigating emotions constructively.

Unaddressed feelings accumulate like unpaid debts, eventually overwhelming your emotional ledger. Regularly addressing these emotions prevents this buildup.

Building Resilience Through Mindfulness

Mindfulness is a powerful tool for emotional resilience. By focusing on the present moment, you reduce stress and gain clarity about your emotional state.

For example, practicing mindfulness during meals— savoring each bite—transforms a mundane activity into a restorative experience. This practice fosters gratitude and strengthens emotional reserves.

Balancing Give and Take: The 50/30/20 Rule of Emotions

Adapted from financial planning, the 50/30/20 rule offers a framework for emotional budgeting:

- **50% Necessities**: Invest in essential relationships and commitments, such as family bonds, close friendships, or

meaningful work. These areas provide emotional stability and fulfillment.
- **30% Discretionary Spending**: Allocate time to activities or relationships that bring joy but are not strictly necessary, like hobbies or casual social interactions. Be mindful of overspending in this category.
- **20% Savings and Debt Repayment**: Dedicate energy to personal growth, healing past wounds, and building emotional resilience. These investments may not offer immediate gratification but yield long-term benefits.

Regularly review your emotional allocations to ensure they align with your priorities. Adjust as needed to maintain balance across these categories.

Fostering Equality in Relationships

Healthy relationships thrive on emotional equality, where both parties contribute and benefit in meaningful ways. When one person consistently over-gives or over-takes, the relationship becomes imbalanced, leading to resentment or dependency.

Recognizing Imbalances

Reflect on your relationships: Are you consistently giving more than you receive, or relying too heavily on others for support? Identifying these patterns is the first step toward creating balance.

For example, if you are always the one initiating plans or offering emotional support, consider whether the relationship is reciprocal.

Encouraging Reciprocity

Reciprocity strengthens relationships by fostering mutual respect and trust. For instance, if a friend frequently confides in you, take the initiative to share your feelings as well. This mutual exchange deepens the connection.

Advocating for Your Needs

Expressing your needs is essential for maintaining balance. Use clear, non-blaming language to communicate your concerns. For example, say, "I feel overwhelmed when I don't receive help with household tasks," rather than, "You never help me."

Advocating for your needs fosters emotional equality and strengthens the relationship.

Tracing the Path Forward

Emotional budgeting is not about perfection but intentionality. It requires ongoing reflection and adaptation as life evolves. By spending energy wisely, setting boundaries, prioritizing self-care, and fostering equality, you create a sustainable emotional framework that supports growth and connection.

Breaking Cycles of Depletion

For those accustomed to over-giving or neglecting self-care, emotional budgeting offers a path to balance. By addressing these patterns, individuals reclaim control over their emotional resources and create space for personal fulfillment.

Building Emotional Wealth

Emotional budgeting not only prevents depletion but also builds wealth. Investing in meaningful relationships, restorative practices, and personal growth creates a surplus of emotional energy that enriches every aspect of life.

Moving Forward

The art of emotional budgeting equips you to navigate life's complexities with balance and intention. By spending emotional energy wisely, protecting your reserves with boundaries, investing in daily self-care, and fostering equality in relationships, you cultivate a framework for enduring well-being.

In the next chapter, we will explore strategies for diversifying emotional portfolios, ensuring adaptability and resilience in the face of life's inevitable challenges.

CHAPTER 12

Diversifying Your Emotional Portfolio

The Value of a Diversified Emotional Portfolio

Life's uncertainties demand a robust and adaptable emotional foundation. Just as financial diversification ensures stability in volatile markets, a diverse emotional portfolio equips individuals to navigate life's complexities with confidence and strength. By broadening relationships, fostering resilience, balancing emotional risks, and preparing for crises, we can cultivate a secure and fulfilling emotional life.

This chapter offers a framework for creating a dynamic emotional portfolio, exploring strategies to enrich relationships, build resilience, and prepare for life's inevitable challenges.

Cultivating a Range of Relationships

Relying on one or two connections for emotional support can leave us vulnerable. A well-rounded emotional network ensures stability and growth, much like diversified financial investments.

The Role of Varied Relationships

Each relationship in your life serves a unique purpose. Some connections, like a childhood friend or sibling, provide grounding and history. Others, such as mentors or colleagues, challenge and inspire growth. Then there are casual relationships— neighbors or acquaintances—that add lightness and variety to your emotional world.

For example, while a best friend may offer deep emotional support, a mentor might guide your professional development, and a neighbor could bring camaraderie through simple daily interactions. Together, these connections create a well-rounded network.

Reassessing Your Emotional Network

To diversify your emotional portfolio, begin by assessing your current relationships. Ask yourself: Are there areas where I am overly reliant on one person? Are there gaps in the types of connections I maintain?

For instance, if you have close family ties but no professional mentors, consider joining a networking group or seeking out guidance in your field. Similarly, if your relationships feel overly serious, cultivating lighter, more casual connections can bring balance.

Building Intentional Connections

Expanding your network does not require forming countless new relationships. Instead, focus on quality over quantity. Look for connections that complement and enrich your existing emotional world.

Take steps to nurture dormant relationships or seek out new ones by joining community activities, volunteering, or participating in shared-interest groups. Each interaction can add a unique layer to your emotional ledger.

Developing Emotional Resilience

Resilience—the ability to adapt and recover from setbacks—is the cornerstone of a strong emotional portfolio. By cultivating resilience, we build the capacity to navigate life's challenges without depleting our emotional reserves.

Adopting a Growth Mindset

A growth mindset reframes obstacles as opportunities for learning. For example, a failed project or relationship is not a definitive setback but a chance to refine your skills or reassess your needs.

To foster this perspective, ask yourself: What can I learn from this situation? How can I use this experience to grow? These questions encourage adaptability and reduce the fear of failure.

Strengthening Inner Resilience

Resilience begins within. Cultivate self-awareness by reflecting on your emotions and recognizing patterns that may hinder growth. Combine this awareness with self-compassion, treating yourself with kindness during challenging times rather than succumbing to self-criticism.

For instance, if you experience rejection, acknowledge your feelings without judgment and remind yourself of your intrinsic worth. These practices fortify your emotional foundation.

Leaning on Support Networks

Resilience is not built in isolation. Surround yourself with trusted individuals who offer encouragement and perspective.

Whether it is a friend who listens without judgment or a mentor who provides guidance, these relationships remind you that challenges are shared and surmountable.

Balancing Emotional Risk and Stability

Emotional growth often requires taking risks—opening up, pursuing new opportunities, or confronting fears. Yet, these risks must be balanced with stability to maintain long-term emotional health.

Embracing Calculated Risks

Emotional risks, such as expressing vulnerability or addressing unresolved conflicts, often lead to growth. For example, sharing a deeply personal fear with a trusted partner can deepen intimacy and understanding.

These risks, though uncomfortable, are vital for meaningful relationships and personal development. Approach them incrementally, starting with small steps that build confidence.

Creating Anchors of Stability

Stability provides the foundation for emotional risk-taking.

This might include maintaining a consistent routine, nurturing reliable relationships, or setting clear boundaries. For example, weekly calls with a close friend can offer grounding support amid life's uncertainties.

Avoiding Overextension

Taking on too many risks simultaneously can lead to burnout. Recognize your limits and focus on manageable steps. For instance, instead of tackling multiple emotional challenges at once, prioritize one area and approach it with intention.

Preparing for Emotional Crises

No matter how carefully curated, every emotional portfolio will face challenges. Preparing for crises—loss, betrayal, or unexpected change—ensures you can navigate them with resilience and grace.

Building an Emotional Emergency Kit

An emotional emergency kit includes tools and strategies for managing stress during difficult times. Components might include:
- A list of supportive individuals you can call.
- Stress management techniques like deep breathing or meditation.
- Journaling prompts to process emotions.
- Affirmations or reminders of your past resilience.

Having these resources readily available can ease the immediate impact of crises and support long-term recovery.

Strengthening Coping Mechanisms

Develop healthy coping mechanisms before crises arise.

This could involve physical activities like yoga or running, creative outlets such as painting or writing, or mindfulness practices like meditation.

Avoid unhealthy habits, such as overworking or substance use, which may offer temporary relief but exacerbate emotional strain over time.

Fostering Emotional Flexibility

Flexibility allows you to adapt to changing circumstances.

For example, if a career setback disrupts your plans, focus on opportunities it may create—like exploring new skills or paths. By remaining open to change, you transform challenges into stepping stones.

Tracing the Patterns

As you diversify your emotional portfolio, patterns rooted in earlier life stages may emerge. Unresolved fears, dependency, or avoidance behaviors can resurface, influencing your ability to form and sustain connections.

Recognizing Limiting Patterns

Identify behaviors or beliefs that limit your emotional growth. For instance, if fear of rejection prevents you from pursuing new relationships, take small steps to challenge that fear—such as initiating a conversation with an acquaintance.

Breaking the Cycle

Replace limiting patterns with constructive behaviors. This might mean practicing self-compassion, seeking therapy, or engaging in reflective journaling to address unresolved issues.

Each step builds confidence and fosters growth.

Revisiting and Refining Your Portfolio

Diversifying your emotional portfolio is not a one-time endeavor but an ongoing process. As relationships evolve and life circumstances change, revisit your portfolio to ensure it aligns with your current needs and priorities.

Balancing High-Yield and Stable Investments

Some relationships are high-yield—demanding but deeply rewarding—while others offer steady, reliable support. Evaluate the balance of these dynamics in your life. Are you overinvested in intense relationships at the expense of stability? Or have you avoided growth by prioritizing only safe connections?

Adjust your investments to create a balance that supports both personal growth and emotional security.

Proactively Managing Emotional Risk

Just as financial markets show warning signs before downturns, our emotional lives often give clues before crises. Pay attention to early indicators, such as feelings of burnout or recurring conflicts, and address them proactively.

By building resilience, strengthening support networks, and practicing self-care, you reduce the impact of life's disruptions and enhance your ability to recover.

Moving Forward

Diversifying your emotional portfolio is a lifelong journey that fosters resilience, adaptability, and fulfillment. By broadening your relationships, building inner strength, balancing risks with stability, and preparing for crises, you create a dynamic framework for emotional prosperity.

As you move forward, revisit your portfolio regularly, making adjustments to align with your evolving needs and priorities. Each relationship, challenge, and triumph enriches your emotional ledger, ensuring that it remains robust and fulfilling through all of life's seasons.

In the next chapter, we will explore emotional entrepreneurship—strategies for creatively deepening connections and expanding emotional wealth to enrich both your life and the lives of those around you.

CHAPTER 13

Emotional Entrepreneurship

The Art of Emotional Entrepreneurship

Emotional entrepreneurship is the practice of actively cultivating relationships, seizing opportunities to deepen connections, and innovating strategies that enhance emotional well-being. It mirrors the entrepreneurial spirit of creativity and purpose, but its focus is human connection rather than profit. By balancing risks and rewards, developing innovative practices, and expanding networks with intention, emotional entrepreneurship empowers individuals to thrive emotionally.

This chapter provides a guide to identifying emotional opportunities, embracing innovation, navigating risks, and scaling up emotional capacity to build a fulfilling and resilient emotional life.

Identifying Opportunities for Emotional Growth

Entrepreneurs seek untapped opportunities in markets; emotional entrepreneurs do the same in their relationships. Growth begins by identifying gaps in your emotional landscape and approaching them with curiosity and courage.

Recognizing Hidden Opportunities

Opportunities for emotional growth often emerge in everyday moments. A brief interaction with a stranger, a supportive comment to a colleague, or an unexpected challenge in a friendship can open doors to connection and self-discovery.

For example, instead of treating a routine meeting as purely transactional, consider asking a colleague about their day or sharing a personal insight. These small shifts build trust and deepen relationships over time.

Turning Challenges into Growth

Conflict and discomfort are often disguised opportunities. A disagreement with a loved one can strengthen communication, while a failure at work might uncover areas for personal development. By approaching challenges with an open mind, you transform obstacles into stepping stones.

Assessing Your Emotional Landscape

Take an inventory of your current relationships and emotional habits. Are there areas where you hold back, overextend, or disengage? Pinpoint patterns that limit growth and explore how small adjustments—like opening up or setting boundaries—could yield meaningful results.

Innovating Emotional Practices

Innovation fuels growth, whether in business or relationships. Emotional innovation involves experimenting with new approaches to connection, communication, and conflict resolution to keep relationships dynamic and fulfilling.

Reimagining Emotional Expressions

Traditional expressions of care, like a quick "thank you" or a routine check-in, often lack depth. Innovate by personalizing these gestures—writing a heartfelt note, creating a shared playlist, or planning a surprise that reflects the recipient's unique preferences.

These thoughtful acts demonstrate intentionality and can transform routine interactions into meaningful moments.

Adopting Creative Communication Tools

Miscommunication is a common source of tension in relationships. Address it by incorporating creative tools to foster clarity and understanding:

- **Active Listening Exercises:** Dedicate time to listening without interrupting or offering solutions.
- **Shared Journals:** Use a notebook or digital app to exchange thoughts or feelings that are easier to write than to say.
- **Check-In Rituals:** Schedule regular times to share updates about feelings, goals, and needs.

Creating Rituals for Connection

Rituals strengthen relationships by adding structure and intention to shared time. Whether it is a weekly family dinner, monthly gratitude journaling, or an annual friendship retreat, these practices anchor relationships in consistency and shared values.

Risk and Reward in Deep Connections

Building deep relationships involves navigating vulnerability and trust—both of which carry inherent risks. The rewards of authentic connection, however, often far outweigh the risks.

Embracing Emotional Risks

Opening up emotionally can feel daunting but is essential for meaningful relationships. Vulnerability fosters intimacy and trust by inviting others to see your authentic self.

For instance, sharing your fears with a trusted partner deepens your bond, even if it feels uncomfortable initially.

Calculating Risks Wisely

Not all risks are worth taking. Assess the potential costs and benefits before opening yourself up or addressing sensitive issues. Consider whether the risk aligns with your values and goals and if it has the potential to enrich your life or relationship.

Learning from Failures

Not every risk yields a reward, and that is okay. Failed attempts at connection or conflict resolution offer valuable lessons. Use these experiences to refine your approach and strengthen your resilience for future endeavors.

Scaling Up Emotional Capacity

In business, scaling up means expanding reach and capacity. Emotionally, it involves deepening existing relationships while fostering new ones, creating a robust and dynamic support system.

Strengthening Core Relationships

Scaling up does not mean spreading yourself thin. Begin by nurturing your most important connections—family, close friends, and mentors. Invest time, express gratitude, and address unresolved conflicts to build a strong foundation.

Expanding Your Network

To grow emotionally, cultivate diverse connections that challenge and inspire you. Join community groups, attend networking events, or reconnect with dormant relationships. Each new bond adds depth and perspective to your emotional portfolio.

Balancing Depth and Breadth

While expanding your network is valuable, prioritize depth over breadth. A few meaningful relationships often provide greater emotional enrichment than numerous superficial ones. Focus on connections that align with your values and offer mutual support.

Managing Risks and Preparing for Crises

Even the best emotional entrepreneurs face setbacks.

Preparing for emotional crises ensures you can navigate them with resilience and grace.

Building an Emotional Emergency Kit

Equip yourself with tools and strategies to manage stress during challenging times:

- **Support Network:** Maintain a list of trusted individuals you can lean on.
- **Self-Care Practices:** Identify activities that help you recharge, like journaling, exercise, or meditation.
- **Affirmations:** Use positive reminders of your strength and resilience.

Strengthening Coping Mechanisms

Develop healthy habits for managing stress and conflict.

Avoid unhealthy coping strategies like withdrawal or overindulgence and instead prioritize practices that promote clarity and balance.

Staying Flexible

Flexibility is key to navigating uncertainty. When faced with unexpected challenges, adapt your plans, and focus on new opportunities rather than clinging to old expectations.

Tracing Patterns and Breaking Cycles

Emotional entrepreneurship often reveals patterns rooted in past relationships or experiences. Addressing these patterns is essential for sustainable growth.

Identifying Limiting Patterns

Recognize behaviors or beliefs that hinder your ability to connect authentically. For example, a fear of vulnerability may stem from past rejection. Gradually challenge these patterns by taking small emotional risks in safe environments.

Reframing Past Experiences

View past failures or disappointments as opportunities for growth rather than permanent losses. This mindset fosters resilience and empowers you to approach future connections with optimism.

Revisiting Emotional Entrepreneurship

Emotional entrepreneurship is a dynamic process that evolves with your relationships and priorities. Regularly reflect on your emotional ledger, identifying areas for growth and celebrating successes.

Ask yourself: Am I approaching my relationships with intention and innovation? How can I continue to refine my emotional investments to align with my values and aspirations?

Moving Forward

Emotional entrepreneurship invites creativity, courage, and connection into your relationships. By identifying opportunities, innovating practices, balancing risks, and expanding your emotional network, you create a thriving and fulfilling emotional life.

As you master these principles, the next chapter will guide you in sustaining emotional prosperity, ensuring the growth cultivated here becomes a lasting legacy for yourself and those you care about.

CHAPTER 14

Emotional Sustainability

The Framework of Emotional Sustainability

Emotional sustainability is the practice of maintaining balance, harmony, and resilience in relationships and within oneself over time. It involves intentionality, mindfulness, and cultivating habits that replenish emotional reserves. By treating emotions as renewable resources, adopting ethical giving practices, fostering ripple effects, and planning for the long term, we create a life rooted in connection and fulfillment.

This chapter provides practical strategies to sustain emotional well-being, ensuring your relationships and internal state remain vibrant and enduring.

Creating Renewable Sources of Joy and Fulfillment

Sustainability relies on sources that replenish rather than deplete. Renewable emotional resources—like gratitude, meaningful activities, and mutual relationships—provide consistent nourishment for the heart and mind.

Joy as a Renewable Resource

Unlike fleeting pleasure, joy sustains emotional energy over time. Cultivating joy requires recognizing its sources and intentionally integrating them into daily life.

- **Identifying Joyful Sources:** Reflect on moments that bring you happiness—shared laughter, creative pursuits, or time spent

around nature. Prioritize these activities, ensuring they become routine deposits into your emotional ledger.
- **Practicing Mindful Joy:** Savoring joyful moments amplifies their impact. Pause to appreciate small but meaningful experiences, like a kind gesture or the warmth of sunlight. Mindfulness transforms everyday events into sustaining memories.

Aligning Actions with Values

Engaging in activities that align with your values creates a sense of purpose and fulfillment. For example, volunteering for a cause you are passionate about not only benefits others but reinforces your emotional well-being.

Investing in Mutually Nourishing Relationships

Sustainable relationships are built on reciprocity, where both giving and receiving feel natural. These connections may require effort but yield consistent emotional returns, reinforcing resilience during challenges.

Ask yourself: What practices consistently bring joy into my life? How can I intentionally sustain these sources?

Ethical Emotional Practices: Giving Without Depletion

Generosity is essential for meaningful relationships, but it must be balanced with self-care. Over-giving leads to emotional burnout, while mindful giving sustains both the giver and the receiver.

Boundaries in Giving

Boundaries are the foundation of ethical emotional practices. They ensure that generosity does not come at the expense of your well-being.
- **Recognizing Limits:** Identify situations where giving feels draining. These moments signal a need to reassess how much energy you are investing.

- **Communicating Needs:** Use clear, compassionate language to express your boundaries. For instance, "I'd love to help, but I need time to recharge first."

Mindful and Intentional Giving

Giving should be rooted in authenticity rather than obligation. Ask yourself: Does this act align with my values? Am I giving from a place of abundance, or am I overextending?

- **Empowering Others:** Instead of taking on someone's burdens, support them in building their resilience. For instance, guide a colleague through solving a problem rather than doing it for them.

Sharing Joy

Sharing joy amplifies its impact. Acts of kindness—like surprising a friend with a thoughtful note—create ripple effects, uplifting both the giver and receiver.

The Ripple Effect: How Emotional Prosperity Spreads

Your emotional health does not just affect you—it influences everyone around you. Sustainable emotional practices create ripple effects, shaping relationships, communities, and even future generations.

Modeling Emotional Wellness

Your habits serve as a blueprint for others. For example, practicing patience during conflicts inspires those around you to approach disagreements constructively.

- **Fostering Positive Cycles:** A parent who models mindfulness teaches children how to navigate stress, creating a generational ripple of emotional resilience.

Acts of Kindness and Connection

Small gestures have far-reaching effects. A simple compliment or an expression of gratitude can brighten someone's day and inspire them to spread kindness.

Ask yourself: What ripple effect am I creating in my relationships? How can I use my emotional prosperity to uplift others?

Long-Term Planning: Emotional Retirement Strategies

Sustainability requires planning for the future. Emotional retirement strategies ensure fulfillment and connection even as life circumstances change.

Building Intergenerational Relationships

Connecting with younger generations provides opportunities for mentorship and legacy-building. Sharing life lessons strengthens bonds and creates a meaningful impact.

Personal Pursuits and Passions

As careers or social circles shift, having personal interests ensures continued purpose. For example, cultivating a hobby like painting or gardening offers joy independent of external validation.

Resilience for Challenges

Prepare for future emotional challenges by maintaining strong support systems and practicing self-care. Addressing unresolved issues now minimizes their impact later.

Ask yourself: What steps can I take today to secure my future emotional well-being?

Tracing and Breaking Unsustainable Patterns

Sustainable growth often involves addressing patterns that undermine balance. Reflecting on these tendencies helps reinforce habits that support long-term well-being.

Recognizing Self-Sabotage

Behaviors like over-giving or avoiding vulnerability can erode emotional health. Identify these patterns and replace them with sustainable practices.

Cultivating Positive Habits

Consistency is key to sustainability. Integrate practices like gratitude journaling or regular check-ins into your routine to ensure they become enduring sources of strength.

Creating a Legacy of Emotional Wealth

Your emotional practices have the power to leave a lasting impact. Acts of kindness, mentorship, and shared wisdom create a legacy that extends far beyond your lifetime.

Emotional Endowments

Consider how your contributions—whether through relationships, community involvement, or personal growth—can benefit future generations. For example, starting a family tradition of gratitude creates a ripple effect of positivity.

Ask yourself: How do I want to be remembered emotionally? What legacy of growth and connection am I creating?

Moving Forward

Emotional sustainability is not a finite goal but an ongoing practice. By prioritizing renewable sources of joy, adopting ethical giving practices, fostering ripple effects, and planning for the future, you create a foundation for enduring fulfillment.

As we approach the final chapter, we will explore how to integrate these lessons into a cohesive emotional legacy, ensuring that the growth cultivated here becomes a lifelong source of strength and connection.

CHAPTER 15

Emotional Wealth Ahead
The Future of Emotional Wealth

Emerging Trends in Interpersonal Dynamics

The landscape of human connection is transforming in ways that demand intentional adaptation. As we navigate a world reshaped by technology, cultural exchange, and evolving social norms, emotional wealth depends on our ability to embrace these changes while preserving the core values of empathy, authenticity, and trust.

Authenticity in a Curated World

In an era dominated by social media, where curated images and performative interactions prevail, the hunger for authenticity is growing. Genuine connections require vulnerability—the courage to present our true selves, flaws, and all. Moving beyond surface- level exchanges toward relationships that prioritize honesty and growth creates a richer emotional foundation.

Expanding Relationship Structures

Traditional definitions of family and partnership are expanding to include chosen families, unconventional living arrangements, and diverse relationship models. These shifts emphasize the importance of quality over conformity, encouraging us to invest in relationships that align with our values rather than societal expectations.

Cross-Cultural Interaction

Globalization has made cultural diversity an integral part of relationships. The ability to navigate cross-cultural dynamics with curiosity and empathy is critical for building meaningful connections in this new era.

Ask yourself: How can I embrace authenticity in my relationships? What steps can I take to adapt to evolving interpersonal norms?

Technology and Emotions: Navigating the Digital Frontier

Technology has revolutionized how we connect, offering opportunities for intimacy and collaboration across distances.

However, it also presents unique challenges for building emotional wealth.

Digital Intimacy

Online communication can bridge physical gaps, but it often lacks the depth of face-to-face interactions. To cultivate emotional wealth in digital spaces, prioritize quality over quantity. Focus on meaningful exchanges that deepen connections rather than engaging in superficial interactions.

Social Media and Self-Esteem

Social media's emphasis on comparison can erode emotional well-being. Combat this by curating your digital environment—unfollow accounts that drain your energy and prioritize content that uplifts and inspires.

Tools for Connection and Growth

When used intentionally, technology enhances relationships. Video calls strengthen long-distance connections, while apps for mindfulness or gratitude journaling foster emotional awareness. These tools, when balanced with offline interaction, enrich your emotional portfolio.

Ask yourself: Am I using technology to enhance my emotional connections? How can I engage more mindfully with digital tools?

Global Emotional Intelligence: Bridging Cultural Divides

The increasing interconnectedness of the world requires a broader emotional intelligence—one that embraces cultural diversity and fosters unity.

Understanding Cultural Norms

Cultural values shape how emotions are expressed and understood. For instance, directness in communication may signify honesty in some cultures but could be perceived as confrontational in others. Recognizing these nuances fosters empathy and respect.

Cultural Humility

Emotional intelligence on a global scale involves cultural humility—the acknowledgment that no single perspective is superior. This mindset creates space for meaningful dialogue and mutual understanding.

Leveraging Diversity for Growth

Cross-cultural relationships provide opportunities to learn and grow. Embracing diverse perspectives deepens your understanding of both yourself and the world. Ask yourself: How can I approach cultural differences with openness and empathy.

New Trends in Emotional Unity

The future of emotional wealth depends on our ability to navigate a rapidly changing relational landscape while staying rooted in universal human experiences.

Reprioritizing Depth Over Quantity

In an age of instant connectivity, the value of deeper, more meaningful relationships is gaining prominence. Prioritizing quality over quantity in personal connections enriches your emotional ledger.

Collaborative Communities

The rise of shared living, group initiatives, and cooperative projects highlights the growing importance of community-based emotional wealth. These structures foster mutual support and collective growth.

Intergenerational Connections

Cross-generational relationships are resurging as sources of wisdom and support. Mentorships and family ties bridge age gaps, enriching both younger and older generations.

The Ripple Effect: How Emotional Prosperity Spreads

Your emotional habits influence not only your life but also the lives of those around you.

Modeling Emotional Resilience

Your behavior patience during conflicts, kindness in interactions—serve as a blueprint for others. By practicing emotional resilience, you inspire those around you to do the same.

Acts of Kindness and Generosity

Small, intentional gestures—such as offering encouragement or expressing gratitude—create positive ripples. These actions foster a culture of support and connection.

Generational Legacy

The emotional example you set shapes future generations. Modeling empathy, resilience, and balance creates lasting ripples in your family and community.

The Ultimate ROI: A Life Rich in Meaningful Connections

At its core, emotional wealth is about creating a meaningful return on investment in the form of joy, fulfillment, and deep relationships.

Auditing Your Emotional Ledger

Regularly assessing your emotional portfolio ensures balance. Reflect on whether your relationships are enriching or draining and make adjustments to align with your values.

Leaving a Legacy

Emotional wealth transcends your lifetime through the impact you have on others. Acts of kindness, mentorship, and wisdom-sharing create a legacy that enriches lives beyond your own.

Lifelong Emotional Riches

Emotional wealth is not a finite goal but an ongoing journey. Lifelong learning, adaptability, and intentionality are key to maintaining abundance.

Adapting to Life's Seasons

Each stage of life presents unique emotional opportunities. From building new connections in youth to fostering legacy in later years, adapting to these shifts ensures sustained growth.

Celebrating Progress

Recognize and honor the strides you have made in your emotional journey. Celebrating small victories reinforces resilience and motivation.

Sustaining Emotional Balance

Consistence in practices like mindfulness, gratitude, and connection builds reserves of emotional wealth that sustain you through life's challenges.

Moving Forward

The future of emotional wealth lies in our ability to embrace change while staying anchored in timeless principles. By leveraging technology, fostering cultural empathy, and prioritizing lifelong growth, you ensure that your emotional reserves remain abundant for yourself and others.

As we conclude, remember that your heart's ledger is a living record of your journey. By continuing to invest in connection, balance, and growth, you create a legacy that reflects not just transactions but transformation.

CONCLUSION

Balancing the Ledger, Enriching Life

Reflecting on the Emotional Journey

The journey through *The Heart's Ledger* has been one of introspection, healing, and transformation. Our emotional lives are shaped by the imprints of our past, the relationships of our present, and the aspirations for our future. Finalizing the emotional ledger is not about closing it but about creating space for reflection, balance, and forward momentum.

Tracing the Past to Understand the Present

Every stage of life—childhood, adolescence, adulthood— leaves traces on our emotional ledger. Parental dynamics, friendships, and societal expectations create patterns that influence how we connect with others. Recognizing these origins is not about assigning blame but about finding clarity. For instance, a deep-seated fear of rejection may stem from early experiences of exclusion. Awareness allows us to rewrite these narratives, choosing trust over avoidance.

Celebrating Progress and Learning from Setbacks

Each relationship and experience, whether harmonious or fraught, provides invaluable lessons. A failed partnership might illuminate the importance of boundaries, while a thriving friendship showcases the power of reciprocity. Reflecting on these moments reframes losses into gains, enriching our emotional reserves with resilience and wisdom. Ask yourself: What lessons have I learned from past relationships? How can I honor these insights as I move forward?

The Ongoing Process of Emotional Accounting

Emotional accounting is not a one-time task but a lifelong practice. It involves regular audits, proactive management, intentional investing, and the flexibility to adapt as life evolves.

1. Regular Audits: Checking the Balance Sheet

Set aside time to review your emotional ledger. Are your relationships enriching or depleting? Are you balancing giving and receiving? These check-ins ensure that your emotional investments align with your values and priorities.

2. Proactive Debt Management: Addressing Imbalances

Unresolved conflicts and unmet emotional needs accumulate like interest on a debt. Address these promptly through forgiveness, amends, or open communication. For instance, if an unresolved argument strains a friendship, initiate a heartfelt conversation to mend the rift.

3. Intentional Investing: Building Emotional Capital

Emotional wealth grows through habits that nurture connection and self-awareness. Practices like gratitude, empathy, and vulnerability compound over time, enriching your relationships and fostering resilience.

4. Adapting to Change: Navigating Life's Shifts

As life evolves, so must your emotional investments. A new phase—such as parenthood, career shifts, or retirement—may require recalibrating how you allocate your energy. Embrace flexibility, recognizing that emotional prosperity depends on adaptability.

5. Seeking Growth Opportunities

Challenges often present opportunities for growth. A difficult conversation, a new relationship, or a personal setback may seem daunting but offers the potential for profound emotional enrichment. Approach these moments with curiosity and courage.

Ask yourself: How am I actively managing my emotional resources? What steps can I take to maintain balance?

Cultivating Emotional Awareness

Self-awareness is the cornerstone of emotional prosperity.

Regular reflection helps you identify your needs, triggers, and patterns, allowing you to navigate relationships with clarity and intention.

Practicing Mindfulness in Emotional Decisions

Mindfulness enables you to respond rather than react. By pausing to assess your emotions, you gain control over your choices. For instance, recognizing feelings of overwhelm early allows you to set boundaries before reaching burnout.

Balancing Self-Care and Connection

Sustainable emotional wealth requires nurturing both yourself and your relationships. Invest in practices that replenish your reserves, such as meditation, creative expression, or physical activity, while maintaining meaningful connections.

Building a Legacy of Deep Connections

Emotional wealth extends beyond individual fulfillment to the legacy we leave behind. This legacy is not measured by material achievements but by the depth of our relationships and the values we impart to others.

Prioritizing Quality Over Quantity

Focus on fostering a few deeply meaningful relationships rather than spreading your energy thin. A long-standing friendship, a close partnership, or a strong familial bond often leaves a more enduring impact than numerous superficial connections.

Sharing Wisdom and Values

Legacy is also about imparting the lessons and principles that have shaped your journey. Whether through storytelling, mentorship, or everyday acts of kindness, you inspire others to carry forward principles of empathy, resilience, and love.

Creating Ripple Effects

The effects of emotional wealth extend beyond immediate relationships. Acts of kindness and generosity create a ripple effect, influencing others in ways you may never see. For example, mentoring a colleague might inspire them to mentor someone else, perpetuating a cycle of growth and support.

Ask yourself: What values and lessons do I want to pass on? How can my actions create lasting impact?

The Ripple Effect: Spreading Emotional Prosperity

Every choice you make in your emotional journey influences others. Your habits of patience, kindness, and resilience serve as a model for those around you, creating ripples of positivity that extend far beyond your immediate circle.

Modeling Emotional Resilience

Your ability to navigate challenges with grace inspires others to do the same. For instance, demonstrating calmness during conflicts encourages those around you to approach disagreements constructively.

Acts of Kindness and Generosity

Small, intentional gestures—like offering a compliment or showing gratitude—create ripples of connection. These seemingly minor actions contribute to a culture of empathy and mutual support.

Lifelong Emotional Riches

Emotional wealth is not static; it evolves with time and effort. Lifelong learning, adaptability, and intentionality ensure that your emotional reserves remain abundant.

Adapting to Life's Seasons

Each stage of life brings unique emotional opportunities.
Embrace these changes as chances for growth. For example, retirement may provide time to deepen family connections or explore new passions.

Celebrating Progress

Recognizing and celebrating your progress reinforces resilience. Each step forward—whether small or significant— contributes to a richer emotional ledger.

The Ultimate ROI: A Life of Fulfillment

The ultimate return on emotional investment lies in a life filled with meaningful connections, personal growth, and lasting impact. Achieving this requires regular reflection, intentional action, and a commitment to fostering relationships that align with your values.

Moving Forward

As we close *The Heart's Ledger*, remember that your emotional journey is ongoing. The lessons, practices, and insights you have gained are tools for continued growth and connection. Your heart's ledger is a living document—a testament to your resilience, love, and purpose.

May your future be marked by deepening relationships, expanding self-awareness, and a legacy of emotional wealth that enriches not only your life but also the lives of others

Glossary

A

1. **Attachment Styles**
   Patterns of bonding shaped by early experiences, influencing trust, intimacy, and conflict resolution in relationships.
   Chapters: 1, 5, 7

2. **Authenticity**
   Showing your true self in relationships, free from pretense or fear of judgment.
   Chapters: 2, 8, 15

B

3. **Blended Families**
   Families formed through the merging of two households, often requiring emotional negotiation and the creation of new bonds.
   Chapters: 10, 13

4. **Boundaries**
   Limits that protect emotional health by defining where your responsibilities end and others' begin, fostering mutual respect.
   Chapters: 4, 11, 14

C

5. **Cultural Humility**
   A mindset recognizing no cultural perspective as superior, paired with openness to learning and adapting to diverse norms.
   Chapters: 10, 12, 15

D

6. **Conflict Resolution**
Constructive strategies to address disagreements, prioritizing understanding, and mutual respect.
Chapters: 4, 7, 13.

7. **Daily Self-Care Practices**
Habits that replenish emotional reserves, such as mindfulness, exercise, or meaningful connections.
Chapters: 9, 11

8. **Diversifying Emotional Portfolio**
Cultivating a variety of relationships and habits to contribute to emotional balance and resilience.
Chapters: 12, 13

E

9. **Emotional Bankruptcy**
Severe emotional depletion caused by prolonged imbalance between giving and receiving.
Chapters: 6, 14

10. **Emotional Capital**
Trust, empathy, and connection as resources that enrich relationships and personal resilience.
Chapters: 9, 13, 14

11. **Emotional Debt**
The unresolved effects of unmet needs, past conflicts, or harm requiring reconciliation and healing.
Chapters: 3, 7, 8

12. Emotional Entrepreneurship
A proactive approach to personal growth and relationships, emphasizing creativity and intentionality.
Chapters: 12, 13

13. Emotional Insolvency
A condition where emotional reserves are insufficient to meet relational demands, often leading to burnout.
Chapters: 6, 14

14. Emotional Ledger
A metaphorical account of emotional gains and losses, shaped by past experiences and present choices.
Chapters: 1, 5, Conclusion

15. Emotional Portfolio
A collection of relationships, habits, and practices that contribute to emotional well-being, balanced between high- yield and stable investments.
Chapters: 12, 15

16. Emotional Sustainability
Practices ensuring long-term emotional health, including self-care, resilience, and ethical relational habits.
Chapters: 9, 14

17. Empathy
Understanding and sharing another's feelings, fostering connection, and reducing misunderstanding.
Chapters: 3, 6, 9.

F

18. Forgiveness
Releasing resentment toward someone who caused harm, fostering personal healing and emotional closure.
Chapters: 7, 8, 13

G

19. Gratitude
The practice of appreciating positive aspects of life, creating emotional resilience and deepening connections.
Chapters: 9, 14

I

20. Ikigai
A Japanese concept of finding a sense of purpose that brings fulfillment and motivation.
Chapters: 12, 15

21. Intergenerational Relationships
Connections across generations that foster wisdom, mentorship, and emotional richness.
Chapters: 10, 15

J

22. Joy as a Renewable Resource
The idea that joy, when cultivated, replenishes itself and serves as a source of emotional strength.
Chapters: 9, 14

L

23. Legacy Accounting
Reflecting on the emotional impact left behind through relationships, values, and contributions to others.
Chapters: 13, Conclusion

R

24. Resilience
The ability to recover from setbacks and adapt to change, enabling emotional stability and growth.
Chapters: 8, 12, 14

25. Ripple Effect
The concept that emotional actions, whether positive or negative, spread outward to influence others.
Chapters: 9, 15

S

26. Self-Compassion
Treating oneself with kindness and understanding during moments of failure or struggle.
Chapters: 8, 11, 14

T

27. Technology and Emotions
The interplay between digital tools and emotional connections, offering opportunities and challenges for relational growth.
Chapters: 13, 15

U

28. Ubuntu
A South African philosophy emphasizing shared humanity and interconnectedness.
Chapters: 12, 15

V

29. Vulnerability
The courage to share one's fears, desires, or insecurities in pursuit of intimacy and trust.
Chapters: 2, 8, 14

References

Bowlby, John. *Attachment and Loss.* Basic Books, 1982. Foundational exploration of how early attachments shape emotional patterns.

Brown, Brené. *Daring Greatly.* Avery, 2012. Examines vulnerability as a cornerstone of meaningful connections

David, Susan. *Emotional Agility: Get Unstuck, Embrace Change, and Thrive in Work and Life.* Avery, 2016. Insights into adapting emotions for resilience and growth.

Goleman, Daniel. *Emotional Intelligence: Why It Can Matter More Than IQ.* Bantam, 1995. Highlights empathy and self-awareness as essential relational skills.

Gottman, John M., and Nan Silver. *The Seven Principles for Making Marriage Work.* Harmony, 1999. Research-backed strategies for nurturing lasting partnerships.

Herman, Judith. *Trauma and Recovery.* Basic Books, 1997. Explores healing past wounds and their impact on emotional health.

Kimmerer, Robin Wall. *Braiding Sweetgrass: Indigenous Wisdom, Scientific Knowledge, and the Teachings of Plants.* Milkweed, 2013. Reflections on reciprocity and emotional balance in relationships.

Neff, Kristin. *Self-Compassion.* HarperCollins, 2011. Guides readers on treating themselves with kindness and understanding.

Perel, Esther. *Mating in Captivity.* Harper, 2006. Explores the tension between autonomy and intimacy in romantic relationships.

Siegel, Daniel J., and Tina Payne Bryson. *The Whole-Brain Child.* Bantam, 2011. Strategies for fostering emotional intelligence in children.

Smith, Emily Esfahani. *The Power of Meaning: Crafting a Life That Matters.* Crown, 2017. Explores the connection between purpose and emotional wealth.

Tannen, Deborah. *You Just Don't Understand.* Harper, 1990. Examines communication styles and their influence on relationships.

Van der Kolk, Bessel. *The Body Keeps the Score.* Viking, 2014. Illuminates the connection between trauma and emotional health.

Yalom, Irvin D., and Ginny Elkin. *Every Day Gets a Little Closer.* Basic Books, 1974. A deep dive into the therapeutic process as a tool for reconciliation and growth.

This curated glossary, index, and reference section serve as a comprehensive guide to understanding and applying the principles outlined in *The Heart's Ledger*. May these tools empower you to deepen your connections and foster emotional prosperity.

Index

A

Accountability in relationships – Chapters 7, 14
Authenticity – Pages 12, 45, 312
Apologies (Sincere) – Pages 178–181
Attachment Styles – Pages 22–25
Auditing Emotional Past – Chapters 1, 6

B

Boundaries for emotional health – Chapters 11, 14
Blended Families – Chapter 10

C

Communication strategies – Chapter 10
Cultural humility – Chapter 13

D

Daily self-care practices – Chapter 11
Debt (Emotional) – Chapters 3, 6, 12
Diversifying emotional portfolios – Chapters 12, 13

E

Emotional awareness – Chapters 8, 14
Emotional capital – Pages 240, 310–315
Emotional entrepreneurship – Chapters 13, 14
Emotional sustainability – Chapter 14

F

Forgiveness practices – Chapter 7

G

Gratitude practices – Chapters 9, 14
Growth as a journey – Conclusion

I

Intergenerational connections – Chapters 5, 15

L

Legacy-building in relationships – Conclusion

R

Reflecting on emotional patterns – Chapters 6, 15
Resilience in emotional crises – Chapters 8, 12

T

Technology and emotions – Chapter 15

www.ingramcontent.com/pod-product-compliance
Lightning Source LLC
Chambersburg PA
CBHW052032030426
42337CB00027B/4969